PRAISE FOR *Imagine* BIG

When I discovered the guitar, my entire life changed. Although I have a God-given talent, it took hours every day of practice for me to play well. I never gave up. I attribute my success to God and hard work. "Believe, achieve and succeed" and "wish it, dream it and do it" . . . these are not my words, but they are the guides I use in my daily life. This book will make it possible for you to change your life if you use it as a guide for your life.

James Burton
Rock and Roll Hall of Fame

The reason I'm such a fan of Terri Savelle Foy is because creativity is a way of life for her. She doesn't just talk about imagination; she lives it. God introduced Himself in the first chapter of Genesis as a cre-ator, and Terri believes that because we are made in His image, the least we can do is live a creative life. I couldn't agree more. It's time Christians embraced real creativity, because that's a critical path to-ward engaging today's culture with a message of hope.

Phil Cooke
Filmmaker, Media Consultant and Author of *One Big Thing: Discovering What You Were Born to Do*

Do you feel like you're stuck in the same place as you were last year at this time? Are you having trouble seeing yourself in a different location and don't know how you would get there if you could see it? If so, the book was written just for you. Let this book help you see what God has in store for you! His plans for you are far above all you could think or dream. *IMAGINE BIG* will open your eyes to a new beginning, a new plan and a new future!

John Copeland
CEO of Kenneth Copeland Ministries International

We can't have it until we can imagine it! Can you see yourself driving that new car, paying off your house, or getting that promotion at work? If not, it's never going to happen. In this important new book, Terri shows step by step how to dream it and then capture those dreams. You owe it to yourself to read *IMAGINE BIG* and take your imagination to the next level in every area of your life.

Chris A. Goodman
President and CEO of OpenRoad Lending

I've known Terri for most of her life, and I've watched her grow up in the Word. She has become a faithful servant and minister of the gospel, and I appreciate her ministry greatly. I believe this book will bless you.

Mac Hammond
Pastor of Living Word Christian Center

Terri's message in *IMAGINE BIG* is as relevant for the student as it is for the CEO. The ability to imagine creates the foundation to accomplish anything. This is a must-read book for anyone who wants the keys to take their life, organization or business to greater levels of influence.

Tara Bollinger Jacob
Co-founder and Director of Jacob Charitable Alliance
Miss Missouri USA 2003

The epitome of every powerful and successful venture in my life has come from the mental integration and spiritual pulling of what Terri Savelle Foy poetically positions within *IMAGINE BIG*. As an authority in the space of personal development and human performance, I can tell you that you're holding a secret to your *breakthrough*!

Ron Kardashian
Celebrity Life Coach and Author of *30-Second Solution*

With her petite frame and soft voice, Terri may not be designed to break bricks with the Power Team, but don't be fooled. On the inside, her passion for God, coupled with her revelation of Scripture, stands a spiritual giant ready to teach you how to *imagine big* so you can break down the barriers between you and your dreams!

Todd Keene
President of The Power Team

IMAGINE BIG is a modern-day guide to success that will inspire you to achieve your highest and most elusive goals. Terri's style of talking about the common day-to-day situations we all experience will show you how to draw on your faith to make your dreams a reality.

Bruce Migliaccio
COO and CFO of Fashion Industry

This step-by-step guide will encourage, inspire and teach you how to fulfill your greatest dreams and goals. It will show you how successful people think and the secrets to their success. Terri shares the practical applications that are needed to accomplish what some might say is impossible. She will motivate you to dream big so you can and fulfill your God-given destiny. A must have!

Sandi Castro Migliaccio
Co-founder and Producer of Safe Passage Pictures

Terri has a unique way to wake up the Body of Christ to dream big dreams. This insightful book will encourage, challenge and inspire you to use your faith to accomplish anything you can imagine by taking off all the limits. No dream is too big when you integrate your faith and overcome the boundaries with vision.

Judy L. Pogue
Motivational Speaker and Co-owner of Pogue Construction

In *IMAGINE BIG*, Terri gives you practical steps to stretch your imagination and help you discover your dreams. This book woke me up from my autopilot life and rekindled the dreams hidden in my heart. Thank you, Terri.

Pam Winters
Owner and Founder of Leadership Team Development, Inc.

Terri Savelle Foy

Imagine
BIG

UNLOCK THE SECRET
TO LIVING OUT YOUR DREAMS

Printed in the U.S.A.

Library of Congress has cataloged the original addition of this work as follows.
Foy, Terri Savelle.
Imagine big : unlock the secret to living out your dreams / Terri Savelle Foy.
p. cm.
Includes bibliographical references (p.   ) and index.
ISBN 978-1-9421-126140 (hard cover : alk. paper)
1. Dreams—Religious aspects—Christianity. 2. Imagination—Religious aspects—Christianity. 3. Success—Religious aspects—Christianity. I. Title.
BR115.D74F69 2012
248.4—dc23
2012030407

CONTENTS

Imagine

BIG

INTRODUCTION

Your imagination is everything. It is a preview of life's coming attractions.
ALBERT EINSTEIN

Your imagination is your ability to envision your future. It's the starting point to bring your God-given dreams to reality. I've written *IMAGINE BIG* to challenge you to stretch your imagination and open your mind to the new possibilities God wants to bring your way. But I won't stop there, because it isn't enough to picture great things in your mind. I will teach you how those imaginings can come to life. When what you see in your imagination is bigger than what you see in your reality, you will begin to attract the ideas, opportunities, resources, faith and relationships necessary to pursue those dreams.

Through the use of powerful biblical examples, personal experiences and inspirational anecdotes, I will unpack the words I.M.A.G.I.N.E. and B.I.G., used like an acronym to show you 10 faith-filled, practical and motivational principles. Each of the 10 chapters in this book focuses on a specific action step from this acronym that will help you see, pursue and live out the deepest visions God has for your life—for your family, your church, and even your community.

Imagine your future
Make a dream book
Assign time daily to review your dreams
Get goals in place
Initiate action now
No more negativity
Express gratitude

Be led by your God-given desires
Invest in your dreams
Get your expectancy high

Cultivating your imagination is vital to shaping your life; and faith is a big part of doing that. Many of us had that child-like faith that Jesus advocated, but we have allowed it to dissipate. We've permitted the realities of life to diminish our capacity to imagine, to dream, to believe. In some cases, it has disappeared altogether.

A friend of mine shared a story that makes the point. He was in Honolulu when he spotted a magnificent mansion that overlooked Diamond Head and Waikiki Beach. He thought, *I couldn't imagine living in a house like that!* At that moment, he heard the Lord quietly respond, *Don't worry about it, son, you never will.* Wow! Those sounded like harsh words, but there is a good lesson here. Your imagination has everything to do with what you will experience in your life. My friend had lost the capacity to imagine big. If we cannot imagine, guess what? Nothing will happen.

Imagining big isn't only true for big houses—it's also a necessity for every dream our big God has for us. It could be that we are moved by the homeless person we see on the street. Maybe we want to write a book that will glorify God and change lives. Perhaps we want to start a small business or become a college professor. Are we willing to imagine the possibilities? If not, guess what? Nothing will happen.

When God inspires and stretches your imagination, you begin to think bigger than you've ever thought before. You begin to enlarge your ability to believe for the impossible. You begin to grow your desire to believe even for what may seem like a pipe dream.

What types of God-given possibilities can you imagine? Can you see yourself giving $100,000 to a cause that tugs at your heart? Building a ministry of worldwide influence? Going back to school to get your master's degree (and actually finishing)? Can you imagine vacationing in Paris, Venice or Sydney? Buying and decorating your dream house? Building a company with thousands of employees? Becoming a fashion mogul? Having the funds to adopt and care for several orphans? Seeing your children commit their lives to the Lord? Creating a nonprofit organization that will feed and clothe thousands of people in need?

I know how hard it can be in today's world to envision a future that is successful, purposeful, prosperous, stable, meaningful and even lucrative. You may think today is not the time to imagine. Life is too hard. Dreams are too unrealistic. Too impossible. The truth is, you cannot allow what is happening in the natural—no matter how bad your circumstances look—to dictate what you imagine, and more importantly, what God can imagine for you.

IMAGINE BIG will inspire you to stop procrastinating and to act now. I believe we tend to get a "tomorrow" mentality about the things we feel God has placed in our dream vision. Many people get stuck thinking the future is far off. We make ourselves feel better when we say, "Someday, I'm going to do that." "Someday, I'm going to get my act together and live for God." "Someday, when I make enough money, I'll spend more time with my kids." "Someday, when my schedule slows down, I'm going to get involved at church." "Someday, when I have more time, I'll focus on getting in better shape." Here's a sobering wakeup call—*someday* won't ever happen unless you act today. Let me show you how *someday* can turn into *today*.

I wrote *IMAGINE BIG* so that you can . . .

- embark on a journey to think bigger than you've ever thought before,
- awaken the dreams that have been buried for too long,
- quit making excuses and start imagining,
- let go of fear and hold on to faith,
- take action to make impossibilities possible, and
- start living God-inspired dreams.

If you want to dream, and expand your imagination, but you are afraid; if you have an active imagination but need direction to actualize your dream; if you need practical steps to turn "what if" into "what is"; if you need encouragement that God can still use your imagination to bring great things to life, then this book will put you on that path and equip you for the journey.

I like the quote from Dexter Yager: "You will never leave where you are until you decide where you'd rather be." *IMAGINE BIG* is the starting point for everything you want, and everything God intends you to be and do.

Chapter 1

IMAGINE YOUR FUTURE

I can teach anybody how to get what they want in life. The problem is I can't seem to find anybody who can tell me what they truly want.
MARK TWAIN

Do you know how to *imagine*?

What does "imagine" mean, anyway? It is defined as "to form a mental image of . . . (something not present)." And what is "imagination"? It's the "creative ability; the thinking or active mind."[1] It is what happens in your mind when you give it room to create. It is what your mind does when you let it come *alive*.

Can you imagine building your dream home? Can you imagine owning your dream car? Can you imagine learning a new language like Spanish and traveling to Spain? Can you imagine going on safari in Africa? Can you imagine owning your own business? What about publishing a book and having hundreds of people come to your book signing to see *you*? Can you imagine having millions of dollars to deposit into your bank account? Or standing in front of thousands of people to perform, preach or give a motivational seminar? Maybe those are your wildest dreams. Maybe you see them as nice little fantasies, but not worth occupying your mind. My goal, through the means of this book, is to help you explore your imagination, learn how to access it and discover God's full potential for you through it.

The *I* in *IMAGINE BIG* stands for "imagine your future." What can you imagine?

We read in 2 Corinthians 4:18, "So we fix our eyes not on what is seen, but on what is unseen, since what is seen is temporary, but what is unseen is eternal." In other words, as believers we are to fix our eyes on the unseen things that God has said are true for our lives, on His promises, His plans and His vision for us. I want you to take this verse to heart, and as you read this book understand that this is what it means to imagine. We can't see the future. We can't see what's coming down the road. But we can have faith in the fact that God has great plans for us.

Start dreaming the dreams that God wants to give you, and devote time to using your imagination according to His desires for you. You may be thinking, *How do I use my imagination? I haven't done that since I played with dolls when I was five.* Well, imagining isn't just playing pretend. It serves a much greater purpose than making playtime fun for kids. The first step is to sit quietly and think. Ask the Holy Spirit to fill you with God's thoughts for your life. In Jeremiah 29:11, the Lord says, "For I know the thoughts that I think toward you . . . thoughts of peace and not of evil, to give you a future and a hope" (*NKJV*). As you sit quietly, see what comes to your mind and let that grow into a dream. Begin to see yourself doing something that seems impossible or out of reach. Once you're able to imagine it, you are one step closer to having what you are visualizing.

It can be downright hard to get a handle on God's dreams for your life, much less pursue them. In this chapter, you will read several inspirational stories and some of my personal experiences that will give you examples of what it means to imagine a better life. I am going to talk about your God-given dreams, your vision and your goals. You will start visualizing what you want in life. I believe that God places things in our hands at certain times to help us get focused on what He wants us to do and where He wants us to go. I believe this book may be the tool you need to resurrect your imagination.

One of my favorite Bible verses is John 17:4: "I have brought you glory on earth by finishing the work you gave me to do." These were Jesus' words before He went to the cross. He perfectly finished a glorious mission that affects everyone for all time who comes to Him. Since He is our role model for life, these words also mean that God has an assignment for every single one of us. He has a mission for me, and He has a mission for you. It will require activating your imagination to find out exactly what that mission is.

Everything Begins with a Vision

I believe that everything we accomplish begins with a vision. One of my passions is to help people get God's vision for their life. You have to see where you're headed before you can start taking productive steps toward it. Before you can do something, you've got to imagine yourself doing it. Before you can have what God wants and what you want, you've got to imagine yourself having it. Before you can be who you're supposed to be, you've got to imagine yourself being it. Napoleon Hill said, "If you do not see great riches in your imagination, you will never see them in your bank balance!"[2]

I recently read a book about success principles. It explained that as a baby you come into this world knowing what you want. When you were an infant, you knew when you were hungry. You knew what food you liked and weren't afraid to spit out what you didn't like. When my daughter, Kassidi, was a baby, I tried feeding her a lot of different pureed foods—squash, peas, carrots and fruit. She loved bananas and peaches. One day I gave her a little taste of corn. I know some people think it's strange, but I can't stand corn. I just don't like it. Well, when I gave my daughter some, she let me know pretty quickly and clearly she felt the same way. Out it came. I said to her, "I understand, baby, spit it out."

As an infant, you have no reservations about expressing what you like and what you don't like. You have no trouble making your wants and needs known. You cry loudly with no inhibitions when you don't get what you want, until someone comes along to give it to you. As you grow, you crawl around and start moving toward whatever holds the most interest for you. You are clear about what you want, and you go after it without fear. I can remember Kassidi crawling toward our dog's food bowl and digging in. I was horrified, but what can you do? Kids see what they want and head straight for it, sometimes faster than we can register what's coming.

So what happens as we grow up? Somewhere along the way, somebody tells us, "Stay away." "Don't touch that." "Get out of there." "Keep your hands off of that." When you get a little older, people start telling you, "You should be ashamed of yourself." "Stop crying." "Don't be such a baby." As you move into adulthood, you hear people say, "You can't get everything you want simply because you want it." "Money doesn't grow on trees." "Can't you think of anyone but yourself? Stop being so selfish." You hear these statements and start putting limits on yourself. You stop going for what you really want. You stop deciding what you really want. You might even stop dreaming or imagining your life any better than it is. You stay stuck in a reality you don't like.

What If?

Ever hear of the game iMAgiNiff™? I don't know if you've ever played it, but I love it. It's so much fun! It's a simple game that tests how well you know, or think you know, your team-mates. You pick a card that asks you to imagine what the other players are, from a list of provided options. For example, one card might ask you to imagine if your brother were a toy, and decide if he would be a Barbie doll, a chemistry set, a teddy bear, a Transformer or PlayDoh. Or it might suggest you imagine that if your best friend were a type of footwear, would she be flip-flops, ballet shoes, jackboots or stiletto heels. The point of the game is not to be cruel toward the people you're playing with, but to get you to use your imagination and start wondering, *What if?*

When you're a child, it's so easy to use your imagination. You do it all the time. When my sister and I were little, we would imagine we were different characters on the TV show *Gilligan's Island*. I could easily think of myself as Ginger, the redheaded movie star with the sequined dresses and lots of makeup. There was no shame in becoming someone else through our imaginations. There were no limitations on what could be. In fact, to our childlike minds, it was more ridiculous to think these big dreams couldn't happen. As a kid, play, through our imaginations, was natural and normal. But here's the thing: It's just as natural and normal to do this as adults. We have simply forgotten *how* to do it. From this day

19

forward, I want you to start imagining. Let your mind wander to things and places you usually don't let it go, and see where God takes you.

Seeing Success to See Success

Successful people use their imagination to create the future they want. This is not some weird science. This is not New Age-y. This is not creepy or bizarre. This is something that God wants us to do. He tells us so in the Bible.

The Hebrew word translated "meditate" includes the meaning "imagine." God commands us in Joshua 1:8 and Psalm 1:2 to exercise our imagination by meditating on and imagining what God says is true in the Bible.[3] For Joshua and God's people in the Bible, this meant imagining and picturing themselves participating in the great acts of God in Israel's history and imagining themselves doing great things by God's power. For us, that means filling our minds with the plans and imaginations that God desires for us, and then taking the actions God shows us to take (see Jas. 1:22-25, which also speaks of this kind of meditating and imagining what God's Word says about us).

Imagine your future. What great things does God have for you? What is the big plan for your life? What if you had $1 million, what would you do with it? If you could have or do anything you wanted, what would it be? Suppose you could go anywhere in the world, where would you go? Have you even given yourself permission to research that place to see how much it would cost?

Sometimes we assume things are so expensive or impossible that we don't take the time to look into the cost or research it further; it is never more than a mere passing thought. I was listening to a CD series by Keith Moore about imagining your future when his words struck me. He said that when we are asked questions about the future, we usually say something like, "Well, I haven't given much thought to it." Keith said that that's no different than saying, "I'm content to stay where I'm at for the rest of my life."[4] Are you content to stay where you are? Are you content with what you have? Do you wonder if God has more in store for your life?

Every goal, every dream and every success begins on the inside of you. In Genesis 15, when God told Abraham that he would be the father of many nations, He actually had Abraham go outside and then said to him, "Look up at the sky and count the stars—if indeed you can count them. . . . So shall your offspring be" (Gen. 15:5). Abraham would not have come close to counting them all, but God wanted him to get that image on the inside of him so strongly that he could see it happening. Abraham had to see it. That's why God sent him outside to *look* at the stars. In essence, He was telling Abraham, "See your potential. See your future. See your dreams."

The same is true with Joseph, whose story is told in the book of Genesis. Joseph had a dream inside of him as a young boy. God gave him that dream. And that dream is what kept him going through years of heartache, rejection and misery. He held on to that vision until it came to pass. Before it ever happened, Joseph saw his brothers and his dad bowing down before him. He saw himself in a position of leadership and authority. Of course, for quite a long time it didn't look like those things would ever come true. Joseph was tossed into a pit. He was wrongfully accused. He was thrown into prison. But, sure enough, because Joseph held on to that dream—that vision—he eventually ended up sitting on a throne in Egypt next to the pharaoh. And one day his brothers came and bowed down to him just as he saw in his dream. But Joseph had to hold on to the vision—the imagination—that was inside of him.

David is another example. He, too, had a vision. When he faced giant Goliath as a teenager, he remembered how God delivered him from the lion and the bear when he was protecting his sheep. He could picture how he conquered these predators. Then God put it on his heart that he could do the same thing with this Philistine enemy who led an army against the Israelites. He could see himself killing Goliath. David obeyed God, followed his vision and conquered the giant.

What is God trying to show you about your future? If your response is, "Terri, I haven't thought that much about it," then your lack of vision will keep you right where you are. Stuck. You have to see your future on the inside first. When you sit back and let things just happen *to* you, nothing will happen *for* you. It takes creating that mental image, that vision, so you can see what you are striving for.

Drafting a Blueprint for Your Dreams

My goal is to help you develop the blueprint of your dreams so that you can see them and begin building toward them. There's something God wants you to fulfill during your lifetime, and it starts with a dream; it starts with vision. He wants you to get excited about the potential. He wants you to draft a sketch of your dreams and get them on paper so that you are able to see the possibilities come together in front of your eyes. Remember, whatever it is that God has called you to do, He is going to give you a pathway to get there.

Not having a vision is not being connected with God's will for your life. "Where there is no vision . . . the people perish" (Prov. 29:18, *AMP*). If you can't visualize anything about your future, you are not moving toward anything, and you are not fully living—you are perishing. But having a vision, using your imagination, comes straight from God. It means having the right expectancy and the right anticipation about tomorrow.

Earlier, I referenced 2 Corinthians 4:18 in the *New International Version*. I'd like to show you another translation: "Things that are seen don't last forever, but things that are not seen are eternal. That's why we keep our minds on the things that cannot be seen" (*CEV*). I like that because it drives home the point that you should keep your mind on things that cannot be seen—your God-given imagination and dreams—the things that look impossible and may even seem ridiculous.

By creating this mental blueprint, your dreams can become more real to you than what you can see with your natural eyes. God is telling us that we are not supposed to base our faith only on what we can physically see, but on those things that He wants us to see in our minds. When God told Abraham, "Look up from where you are and see the stars," He wanted him to visualize what he could be, but Abraham had to have some kind of mental blueprint to really see it.

When I was a little girl, my parents began instilling in me the idea of developing eyes of faith. They told me I had to see the things I believe for with my spiritual eyes. "Don't be moved by what you see with your physical eye," they said. "Believe that what you see on the inside can happen on the outside." When I was seven years old, I trusted God to provide a piano. My parents actually left a space in our den for my piano and told me, "Act as if it's already there. Every time you walk by this area, walk around it as if you were trying to avoid bumping into a piano." This exercise may sound foolish—and believe me, I felt a little crazy acting "as if"—but it comes straight from the Word of God. And it works. Next, Mom and

23

Dad told me to add another step of faith and point to that empty space and say, "Thank You, Lord, for my piano." I did this every single day.

At one point, when I was starting to feel a little confused, I brought it up to my dad. "I have a piano. You say I have it. It's there. I see it by faith. But how come I can't ever play it?" Daddy replied, "You will, Terri. One day you will be playing that piano. You keep believing." You know what? In a short time, my piano came, and it sat right where I saw it all along. The image began on the inside and then it showed up on the outside.

You need faith to produce your blueprint. Jesus said, "It shall be done to you according to your faith" (Matt. 9:29, *NASB*). This is more powerful than you know. One time, I wrote out a check for $10,000 that I wanted to give to a ministry. I did so by sheer faith. It seemed crazy when I didn't even have $1,000 to give. But I wrote that check as a step of faith, and I put it in my dream book. (That's where I keep all my dreams. We'll cover that in a later chapter.)

I would lay hands on the check, believe in Jesus' name and confess every day that one day I would give $10,000 all at one time to this particular ministry. I did this so many times and believed it that I could actually see myself mailing that check off. God was faithful. He made a way for me to give that amount.

It shall be done to you according to your faith.

According to your faith you will possess the dreams and the desires that you have on the inside. If you have a small amount of faith, you will accomplish small dreams and small desires. The more you develop your faith, and the bigger that faith gets on the inside of you, you can achieve bigger dreams and desires.

Make Up Your Mind

There are some cardinal messages about dreams that I need to make clear. First, God hasn't given you the dreams He has given me, and vice versa. He hasn't given them to the person next to you. He hasn't given them to your spouse or your friends or your neighbors. Those dreams and desires are unique to you; so don't let others make you feel that your dreams are foolish, crazy or ridiculous because they aren't their own dreams. God puts those desires in you for a reason.

Second, just because God has given you a dream doesn't mean it will manifest automatically. You have to make up your mind that you will believe for it no matter what, and then start acting on it. You must persevere, no matter how difficult or uncomfortable it feels.

I'll be honest. I wasn't always good at making up my mind. In fact, years ago I got into a habit of letting other people make decisions for me, even when it came to meals. When I went out to eat with my best friend, I would ask her, "What do I want? Do I want a taco? Pizza? French fries?" How could she possibly know what I wanted to eat? Surprisingly, she sometimes did, and she made the decisions for me (at least for a little while).

You've got to stop settling for less than what you want. Motivational speaker Jack Canfield once said, "One of the main reasons why most people don't get what they want, is they haven't decided what they want. They haven't defined their desires in clear and compelling detail."[5] I know it can be hard to dream again and get in touch with what you want. Canfield suggests honoring your preferences no matter how big or small. He suggests that saying things like, "I don't care," "I don't know" or "It doesn't matter to me" when you are confronted with a choice, no matter how small or insignificant it seems, is giving up control of your own life. Act as if you have

25

a preference, even if you don't. Ask yourself, "If I did know, what would it be? If I did care, which would I prefer? If it did matter, what would I rather do?"

I took his advice and started with the small matters of my life. I decided which movie to rent. I decided where to eat after church on Sunday. I decided where to go on the family vacation. Once I started making those little decisions, I was able to move on to bigger things, like choosing the dreams for my life. When you practice making decisions in small areas, it will lead to making them in big areas.

Not being clear about what you want, and making other people's needs and desires more important than yours, devalues your opinions, your mission and your needs. This is simply a habit—one you can break by practicing the opposite habit.

The Power of Imagination

Don't let your imagination lie dormant and allow yourself to become stuck in the routine of life. That's easy to do, especially as we get older and have more responsibilities. Our dream lists tend to take a backseat to the To-Do lists.

I read recently that when you perform any task in real life your brain uses the same process it would use if it were only vividly visualizing that activity. Your brain sees no difference whatsoever between imagining something and actually doing it. Imagine that! The study went on to explain that using your imagination, or visualizing your dreams first, makes the brain achieve more.

I have seen this principle explained in many books on success. There's even an example in the Bible. Genesis 11 tells the story of the Tower of Babel. The people were trying to build a tower that would reach to heaven. (Can you imagine completing this construction project before concrete mixers, cranes or power tools were invented?) The Lord actually said of their ef-forts, "Behold, they are one people and they have all one lan-guage; and this is only the beginning of what they will do, and now nothing they have imagined they can do will be impossi-ble for them" (Gen. 11:6, *AMP*). Think about that. God said nothing they imagined would be impossible for them. That's the power of imagination.

So where do you start? You begin with an idea, a fragment that eventually grows into a full-blown dream. With determi-nation, faith and practical goal setting, it becomes a reality. Most of us are so busy doing things we have to do that we never get around to doing what we want to do. Or maybe we never take the time to think about what God wants us to do.

I want you to take some time and sit quietly. Ask the Holy Spirit to fill you with His imagination for you. Imagine your life the way God and you want it. That's right. Put this book down and breathe for a moment. Let your imagination run wild. No holds barred. No judgments. Allow yourself the free-dom to imagine. Spend a few minutes visualizing the future you want. (You don't have to sit there for hours.) What do you see? What does your dream look like? Who is there? What are you doing? How do you feel? Where do you live? Which city? Is it by a lake, an ocean or the mountains? What does your house look like? Is it brick, stone, stucco or . . .? What does your office look like? Where do you work—from home, or an office building? What is your ideal salary? What is the exact amount? Can you see that number? Can you give yourself per-mission to dream that big? These are the questions you need to ask yourself. Don't be vague about your future. Vague de-sires bring vague results. Imagine big and in clear detail.

It's a fact that we are creatures of habit. Every day we fol-low the same routines without even thinking about them;

from the way we put on our shoes to the way we take our vitamins; from the way we make our coffee to the route we drive to work. We spend much of our time on autopilot. There are probably 200 different restaurants where you live; but more than likely, you only eat at four or five of them and limit your order options to four or five of the same dishes every time.

It's not until you stop and think about what you're going to do with the rest of your life that change happens. Are you doing the same things you did last year, and wondering why your life is no different? Make decisions that will lead to and support the goals you want to achieve. If you don't like the results you are getting in your life, change what you are doing. Start doing things that lead toward your dream. In the chapters that follow, I will explain what those steps are and give you plenty of pointers to start moving toward your dream.

What do you want out of life? Where do you want to go? Here's a thought: Would you get in your car and drive without knowing where you were going? Probably not. You'd waste time, gas and money. Why wouldn't you have the same approach with your life? We each have a mission—an assignment from God—and we have to know where we are going to accomplish that. Unlock the power of your imagination to help you find your destination.

To Dream the Impossible Dream

When we were children, we imagined constantly and were able to believe anything was possible. It makes me sad how many of us have stopped dreaming and using our imaginations. When Kassidi was young, I suggested she jot down all her dreams in a journal. Some of the dreams she has written down are to own an airplane and a house in the south of France, as well as one in Paris, plus one in a ski lodge area. She has not placed any boundaries on her dreams. I have never thought about saying, "Oh, Kass, that's a bit far-fetched, honey." I wouldn't dare do that. I want her to believe that nothing is impossible with God. If you can dream it, God can do it.

I'm telling you the same thing as I've told my daughter. Get that youthful imagination back in your life. And then find that childlike faith to believe that if God can give you a dream, He can surely bring it to pass.

I read a study from Harvard University where researchers discovered that students who imagine first, perform tasks with nearly 100 percent accuracy; whereas, students who didn't visualize before they started only achieved 55 percent accuracy.[6] This is more proof that using your imagination—visualizing your dreams—isn't a bunch of feel-good nonsense. It works. Almost all Olympic and professional athletes now practice visualizing their intended outcome. In other words, they use their imaginations to train and compete.

In fact, I read recently that Jack Nicklaus, the legendary golfer who has now won more than 100 tournament victories and more than $5.7 million in winnings, said, "I never hit a shot, not even in practice, without having a very sharp, in focus picture of it in my head."[7] Olympic gold medalist and motivational speaker Peter Vidmar said, "To keep us focused on our Olympic goal, we began ending our workouts by visualizing our dream from beginning to end. . . . When we won the gold medal, it was exactly the way we visualized it in the gym."[8]

If you don't know what you want, you'll never find it. You'll never imagine it. There is power in taking time to see beyond where you are right now. For a long time, I never gave a thought to the future. I think I was scared to dream, because I didn't know if I was making stuff up or if it was really God's

29

plan. But know this: Fear is not from God, and dwelling on fear keeps you from fulfilling His purpose for you. So start thinking today about what tomorrow could hold for you.

It's Never Too Late

I have received countless testimonies from people all over the world who have finally given themselves permission to dream. They know that if they can dream it, God can do it. I want you to give yourself permission to dream. I also want you to dream as big as you possibly can. I want you to enlarge your thinking. Start realizing there's so much more to life, so much more to do.

Your life isn't over because you got married and have small kids or grown ones. Your life isn't over because you retired or because you are past a certain age. Your life isn't over, even though you've made mistakes, gone through some hard times or feel broken by life. One more thing: You're not too young to dream big. And it's never too late to live a dream-filled life and do all the things you've always wanted to do.

It's *Never* Too Late

I love this quote by nineteenth-century English novelist George Eliot: "It's never too late to be what you might have been." What a powerful truth! The people I have listed below are no different than you. They just took the necessary steps to pursue what was already in their hearts.

- At 11 months old, Brooke Shields was hired for her first television commercial as the Ivory Snow baby.

- At 4 years old, Shirley Temple began her film career, and three years later received an Academy Award.
- At 8, Mozart composed his first symphony.
- At 11, Michael Jackson sang the smash hit "ABC" with the Jackson Five.
- At 12, Pocahontas saved the life of Captain John Smith.
- At 13, Anne Frank began writing in what would later become a world-famous diary when she and her family were forced into hiding from the Nazis.
- At 15, Justin Bieber became the first artist to have seven songs from a debut album chart the Billboard Hot 100 list.
- At 18, Cassius Clay, later named Muhammad Ali, won the light heavyweight boxing gold medal at the 1960 Olympic games.
- At 18, Tommy Hilfiger opened his first clothing store.
- At 20, Debbie Fields founded Mrs. Fields Cookie Company.
- At 38, Terri Savelle Foy launched her ministry and terri.com.
- At 42, Joyce Meyer launched her worldwide ministry in Fenton, Missouri.
- At 45, Susan Sarandon won the first of three Academy Awards for Best Actress nominations and gave birth to her third child.
- At 45, Henry Ford introduced the automobile called the Model T.
- At 49, Julia Childs wrote *Mastering the Art of French Cooking*.
- At 52, Leonardo DaVinci completed the "Mona Lisa."
- At 56, Gustave Eiffel completed the design for the Eiffel Tower in Paris.

- At 58, Bruce Springsteen and the E Street Band were named Best Live Band of 2008 by *Rolling Stone* magazine.
- At 72, Michelangelo designed St. Peter's Basilica in Rome.
- At 76, Henry Fonda won his first Oscar after 46 years of acting.
- At 83, Winston Churchill completed *A History of the English Speaking Peoples*.
- At 90, Nelson Mandela adorned the cover of *TIME* magazine.
- At 98, Dimitrion Yordanadis ran a marathon in 7 hours and 33 minutes in Athens.
- At 99, Abraham and his wife, Sarah, gave birth to their son Isaac.
- At 100, Teiichi Igarashi climbed Mount Fuji.

32

Start Dreaming

An extremely brilliant writer named Dr. Seuss once said, "You have brains in your head and feet in your shoes. You can steer yourself any direction you choose. You're on your own and you know. And you're the one who'll decide where to go."[9]

Where are you going? Where are you headed? For what are you believing? What are you focused on? What are some of the things you pray about? You may have heard this story about Kenneth Hagin: When he was alive, he would watch people pray at the altar. He'd walk up to them, gently tap them on the shoulder and say, "Excuse me, what are you praying about?" Most of the time their response would be, "Oh, nothing in particular." Brother Hagin would shake his head and reply, "Well, that's exactly what you're going to get—nothing in particular."[10] I don't know about you, but it makes me realize we need to be specific in what we're praying about. We also need to be specific in where we're headed, how we are steering our imaginations. Unless you can visualize something different, you will never move beyond where you are today.

Earlier, I asked you to stop everything and spend some time sitting quietly in thought and allow your imagination to start moving. Did you do that? If not, do it now. Shut the door and turn off your phone, TV, iPod, laptop—anything that makes noise and will distract you. Sit in a quiet space.

Prolific author and speaker John Maxwell said, "Thinking precedes achievement . . . Nobody just stumbled upon success and then tried to figure it all out afterwards. The greater your thinking, the greater your potential."[11] "For as he thinks within himself, so is he" (Prov. 23:7, *NASB*). You have to take the time to think before you start taking steps. Imagine. Wonder. Dream.

I want you to imagine your future. Imagine money in your account. Imagine yourself at your ideal weight. Imagine yourself as a foster parent. Imagine yourself driving your dream car. Imagine yourself teaching a class. Imagine yourself as a youth leader. Whatever your dream, you have to see it. You have to imagine the dreams and visions that God has for you. The late Dr. Benjamin Mays, educator and social activist, made this statement, "It isn't a calamity to die with dreams unfulfilled, but it is a calamity not to dream." Don't let this be the commentary on your life.

Just today, I was going through a stack of testimonies and comments from people who send me emails and write to me. I can't tell you how many of them share how they are passionate about their dreams, but they're hesitant to pursue or believe for them because those dreams seem impossible. I have permission to share with you what one of my readers wrote:

• • • • •

33

• • • • •

Hello Terri, I just want to say thank you for your encouragement. I look forward to your letters each month. Everything you said makes me want to pursue my dreams even harder. Your question of where do I see myself in the next five years made me think and it just makes me want to get busy right now at this moment and go after my dreams. I have so many things I want to accomplish. I want to write a book, start a business, finish college, travel on missionary trips helping the poor and less fortunate. I have so many dreams, but it just seems so impossible at times because I don't have the resources or the right contacts to help me get where I want to be. I've been praying about it, and sometimes I even get angry because I just do not see anything happening. I know God is listening and hears my prayers. I don't know why it's taking so long for it to come to pass. . . . I will not give up, because every time I feel like giving up, something inside of me just will not let me.

Perhaps there are things you're believing God for, but they look so far out of reach. You don't have a clue how God can make them come true. Maybe you think it's foolish to even try to imagine. I know how you feel. Most of the dreams I have seem impossible. I don't know how God can accomplish them. I don't know the right people. I don't have the finances. I don't have the equipment or the personnel. Truth is, I don't know how they're going to happen. All I know is that God told me to dream. But I also have the track record of imagining my future and watching my dreams materialize!

So don't worry if you are imagining things that reach beyond the realm of reality. Don't worry if you can't figure out exactly how they will actualize. Don't worry if they seem impossible. You serve a big God who wants you to dream big. Dream those impossible dreams. It's a sure sign it will require faith in the God who specializes in doing the impossible.

All you have to do is start to imagine.

"I Want" List

Learning to dream again can be difficult if you are out of practice, but it is an important part of becoming reconnected with what you want from life, determining if you are on the path to getting it and finding your dreams.

Here is an activity to stretch your imagination and get you thinking about what you want. Write down a list of 20 things you want to do, have or be. This exercise gives you permission to think and to imagine and to dream beyond where you are right now. Go ahead. Write them down in the space below.

1. _____
2. _____
3. _____
4. _____
5. _____
6. _____
7. _____
8. _____
9. _____
10. _____
11. _____

3 5

12. _____
13. _____
14. _____
15. _____
16. _____
17. _____
18. _____
19. _____
20. _____

· · · · ·

3 6

· · · · ·

Chapter 2

MAKE A DREAM BOOK

Then the LORD told me: "I will give you my message in the form of a vision. Write it clearly enough to be read at a glance."
HABAKKUK 2:2, CEV

In 1990, when Jim Carrey was a young, struggling standup comic trying to make it in Hollywood, he would drive his old Toyota up to Mulholland Drive, look out at the city below and imagine his future. One time he even wrote himself a check for $10 million and postdated it "Thanksgiving 1995." He wrote in the memo, "for acting services rendered." Carrey kept that check (and that dream) in his wallet, and it went with him everywhere.

After the films *Ace Ventura Pet Detective*, *The Mask* and *Dumb and Dumber* were released in 1994 and became huge box office hits, Carrey's asking price had risen to $20 million per picture. When his father died the same year, he placed that $10 million check into his dad's coffin as a tribute to the man who taught him to dream.[1] Isn't that awesome? Carrey walked right into his dreams.

I want to show you the importance of recording what you imagine. Your vision and your dreams must be on paper. How many times have you gone to the grocery store without a shopping list and forgotten an item (or two) you needed? Or you had something to do for your kids but you forgot because you didn't write yourself a reminder? Dreams are no different.

Habakkuk 2:2-3 says, "Then the LORD told me: 'I will give you my message in the form of a vision. *Write it clearly enough to be read at a glance.* At the time I have decided, my words will come true. You can trust what I say about the future. It may take a long time, but keep on waiting—it will happen!'" (*CEV*, emphasis added).

The *M* in *IMAGINE BIG* stands for "make a dream book." In this chapter, I will show you how to create a dream book to inspire you to imagine great things. By taking the time to put your vision down in this creative way, you establish the discipline of remembering your dream, and you will attract the images you keep before your eyes. You have to write what you see. Get your dreams on paper.

For example, if you have a dream of owning a house by a lake, imagine what it looks like and write that down. Be specific. If you see a big deck, a hot tub or lots of trees, write down those details. I suggest making (or finding and cutting out) pictures of similar-looking houses and using those images as a point of reference. If you dream of going back to school and getting your master's degree, make a picture of a diploma with your name on it. If you dream of earning $50,000, get a blank check, write in the dollar amount and put it somewhere you'll always see it—either in your dream book (I will explain this in the next few pages) or on the bathroom mirror or refrigerator or a vision board. The point is, write it down.

I'm telling you from experience, something happens when you put your dreams on paper. It proves you're serious. It confirms that you are committed. It is evidence of how

· · · · ·

38

· · · · ·

badly you want them. You instantly become that much closer to reaching your dreams.

The Power of the Pen (and Paper)

The late Bruce Lee, one of the greatest martial artists who ever lived, understood the power of using his imagination, declaring his dreams and writing them down. If you ever have a chance to visit Planet Hollywood in New York, look on the wall for the letter Bruce Lee wrote to himself, dated January 9, 1970, and stamped "Secret."

Lee made this written promise to himself: "By 1980, I will be the best known Oriental movie star in the United States, and I will have secured $10 million; and in return, I will give the very best acting I can possibly give every single time in front of the camera, and I will live in peace and harmony." Lee made only three films. In 1973, he filmed his last movie, *Enter the Dragon*, which was released that same year after his untimely death at age 33. The movie was a huge success. In only three years, it made millions of dollars and achieved worldwide fame for Bruce. Can you even comprehend that? He did exactly what he wrote. The letter hanging in Planet Hollywood demonstrates the power of writing your dreams.

In 1966, now-retired Notre Dame coach Lou Holtz was out of a job, and his wife was eight months pregnant. It seemed like everything was going wrong for them. One day his wife gave him a book about thinking big. It suggested writing down the dreams and goals you want to achieve in life. Holtz sat down and let his imagination run wild. He listed 107 things he wanted to achieve before he died. The list included shooting a hole in one at golf, having dinner at the White House, appearing on the *Tonight Show* with Johnny Carson, meeting the Pope, coaching at Notre Dame and leading his football team to a national championship.

Lou has achieved 102 things on his original list.[2] Pretty amazing, isn't it? It happened all because of the powerful principle of writing the vision, making it plain on paper. When you take the time to write out your dreams, you are stepping forward into making your imagination become a reality.

Get a Dream Book

Now that I have given examples of the power of putting your dreams on paper, let's go over the most effective way to do that. For many years now, I've written all of my dreams and goals in what I call a dream book. You may have heard of the concept of a vision board. A dream book is basically the same thing, just a different name and a different format.

I used to tell people to buy a three-ring binder and fill it with pages of words and pictures that state, describe or illustrate their dreams. One day it dawned on me that since part of my personal vision is to provide people with the resources they need to help them pursue their dreams, there is no reason I shouldn't produce a dream book. I brainstormed and created what I call "My Personal Dreams and Goals Notebook." You can purchase one (or a few to inspire your friends and family) at www.Terri.com.

This unique notebook will help you to stay focused and organized as you pursue the dreams of your heart. All you have to do is write your dream, find a picture that relates to it, tape it in there and keep the notebook with you as a reminder. I've also included questions and motivational thoughts to stretch your imagination and prompt you to think outside the realm of possibility. I've even written down ideas to help spark your desires.

If you would rather create your own dream book, you can be as crafty or as simple, as elegant or as artistic as you like. You can use a piece of poster board, a corkboard, a basic journal or a spiral-bound notebook. It doesn't matter what your dream book looks like as long as you write down your dreams.

The one rule I do set is that it's imperative to use pictures to support your imaginings. This will help ignite your creativity and motivate you. By searching for actual images, you become more engaged in the active part of dreaming. You begin to see how your dreams can look in real life—*your* real life.

Warning: As you get started, Satan will try to tell you that what you are believing for is impossible. He'll whisper in your ear things like: "You're never going to do this." "You're never going to go there." "You're never going to have that." Don't listen to a word he says. These thoughts are nothing but lies. Instead, continue to give yourself permission to dream. There are so many places God wants you to see, and experiences He wants you to have. But you will only get there if you start dreaming and writing those things down.

What I love most about my notebook is that you can keep all your dreams together. In fact, a gentleman told me the other day, "Terri, I've known for years that in the business world it's important to write my dreams and goals. I've done that, but I have them all over the place. With your notebook, they're all in one place, and I refer to them daily."

Have fun with your dream book, whatever it looks like. Stretch yourself. Get out of your comfort zone. Think big. God has a plan for you, a big one. He has a contribution He has called you to make. He also has created things He wants you to enjoy in your life. If you feel stuck, remember that God has more in store for your life.

41

Start imagining. Start writing your dreams. If your car is older than you are and breaks down every week, and you need it to get to work or to take your kids to school, imagine yourself driving a new car. Take a bold step of faith and head down to the nearest car dealership and take home some brochures of the car you want. Cut out the pictures and put them in your dream book. Imagine yourself owning that car. Imagine yourself pulling out of your driveway, going to work, coming back home and parking your new car in the driveway.

Jesus was known for His miracles. He turned water into wine. He healed people. He walked on water. He calmed the storms. He raised the dead. And yet, He said, "I tell you the truth, anyone who believes in me will do the same works I have done, and even greater works" (John 14:12, *NLT*). He also said, "If you have faith in God and don't doubt, you can tell this mountain to get up and jump into the sea, and it will. Everything you ask for in prayer will be yours, if only you have faith" (Mark 11:23-24, *CEV*). Don't limit what God can do in your life by thinking small or by not dreaming at all. Get a dream book today and write down your dreams.

Have you heard of Marilyn Kentz and Caryl Kristensen, the comedic duo known as The Mommies? Years ago, they had a TV show where they would humorously talk about domestic life, their kids, everyday stresses and motherhood. These women believed in the power of writing down dreams. Marilyn and Caryl, neighbors in the small farm town of Petaluma, California, became fast friends and decided one day to try their luck at performing comedy routines. But before they started out, they made a goals book. They listed all of their dreams and ambitions and used images to illustrate them.

Here's the cool part. Everything they wrote down in the book happened. That's right! Every single thing. These highly accomplished and very funny ladies had two TV shows, *The Caryl and Marilyn Show* and *The Mommies*. They also wrote a very successful book titled *The Mother Load*.[3]

You should see my dream book. I have written down so many things, even small desires, like owning certain pieces of furniture. It may sound silly, but it works. One day, I went on-line and found the bedroom set I've always wanted. It was a beautiful Italian-style bed and armoire; but it was too expensive to buy at the time. I printed out the picture, taped it inside my book, prayed over it and sowed seed for it. I didn't have the money to buy it, but I had the vision. My job was to get the vision on paper, to show God I was serious. I did this with more than furniture. I even dreamed of, wrote down and pasted images of towels for my guest bedroom, types of clothing and dishes. Believe it or not, I have imagined these items in detail, and I own every single one, debt-free. God made a way where there seemed to be none to get the things I was believing Him for.

My notebook is not only filled with dreams about material things. I also write down my dreams that concern others—like expanding my ministry in France by ministering in 20 cities across the country, speaking in the largest success and motivational venues in the U.S., giving thousands of my books away to teenage girls troubled by their past, and so on. Some of my dreams may look impossible, but I am confident they can come true, because God keeps bringing them to pass, one by one. My family, friends and staff are amazed to look at my dream book and see dozens of dreams fulfilled each year.

Remember the man who appreciated the dream book I created because it kept everything in one place? He also said, "Every day before I leave the house, I get my dream book out and I pray over it." Wow! I was so encouraged by his words.

43

You know what? That's exactly what I do—I pray over my book every day. Not once a month. Not once a week. Not every now and then, but every day. It has become a habit. And that's what has kept me focused on achieving these dreams.

The best way to start a habit is by doing it at the same time every day. It's like brushing your teeth. You don't have to place a big note on your bathroom mirror that says, "Brush teeth in the morning" (at least I hope not!). You just do it. I don't need to be reminded to pray over my dream book. I just do it. When I come home from the gym in the morning, I go into my guest bedroom, get out my dreams-and-goals notebook and start picturing my dreams in my mind and speaking them out of my mouth.

This exercise works like a GPS system. When you activate it, all of a sudden you find ways to get to your destination, to achieve your dreams. When you put your dreams and your vision at the forefront of your mind, opportunities for them start appearing. You meet people. Job openings come to your attention. You start turning the corner to your dreams becoming real.

Be Specific

I read a story about a guy named John Assaraf who, in 1995, created a vision board and hung it on a wall in his office. Whenever he dreamed of something material that he wanted, such as a trip he wanted to take or a house he wanted to buy, he would find a photo of it and glue it to the board. Then he could see himself already enjoying the object of his desire.

Five years later, having recently moved into his new home in Southern California, John was in his office one morning when his five-year-old son, Keenan, came in the room. The little boy sat down on a couple of boxes that had been in storage for four years and asked his father what was in the boxes. John told him his vision boards, and Keenan replied, a little bit confused, "Your vision what?"

John opened one of the boxes to show his son what he meant. The man smiled as he looked at the first board that revealed a Mercedes-Benz sports car, a watch and some other items, all of which he had acquired. Then, as he pulled out the second board, John began to cry. On that board was a picture of the very house he had just bought and was living in. I'm not talking about a home similar to it, but the very house—a 7,000-square-foot house with spectacular views that sits on six acres and has a 3,000-square-foot guest house, an office complex, a tennis court and 320 orange trees. John had cut out a photo of this home from a magazine four years earlier. He was living in the actual house he had imagined.[4]

The Bible tells us that nothing is impossible with God (see Luke 1:34). Nothing! Ask God to give you His plans and use your imagination. Dream as big as you possibly can. Give God something to work with. Be specific. Write the desires of your heart. Do these things and you'll find that your dreams will begin to unfold.

Let me clarify something about dreaming. Your dreams are not solely about material things; and sometimes they have little or nothing to do with you. It could be that your dream is to raise godly kids. If that's what you want, imagine your kids worshiping God. Imagine them becoming youth leaders. Your dream could be to start a soup kitchen in your community. Picture a line around the block of people in need being served by your act of obedience. Your dream could be to become a foster parent. Imagine taking that child to school, to the park, and instilling godly principles into his or her life.

· · · · ·

45

· · · · ·

Take a break for a few minutes. Think about these next few questions: What do you see? What can you imagine? What dreams are you anxious to write down? If you're still stuck, remember the exercise I mentioned in the previous chapter. Spend time in quiet. Think about what you want. Think about the dreams God has laid on your heart. This is a habit worth developing. Close your eyes and dream. Imagine yourself living the best life that God has for you. If the dreams that come to mind seem wild and crazy, I'm willing to bet you're on the right track.

Imagine your dreams and write them down. If your dream is to get out of debt, do your homework. Add up the dollar amount of what you owe and write it down in your book. Imagine paying off every one of them. Imagine living a debt-free life.

Don't wait; the time is now. God wants to do so much more in your life, and He can't help you until you see it. So imagine. Dream big. Write. And don't forget the last part of Habakkuk 2:3: "Keep on waiting. It will happen."

Once you've created a dream book, spend some time and look at the pictures you put in there. Use them to help you stay focused. Use them to remind you that your dreams are for real. They are not pipe dreams. They are not wishful thinking. They are not a mere fantasy. They are what you believe God for and what will one day materialize in your life.

Stretch Your Imagination

There is power in putting your dreams to paper. Just taking the time to get a pen requires some action that makes this more than a fleeting thought. But, when you start recording your dreams, you might need to stretch your imagination.

To see your dreams come true, you have to be stretched. Here's what I mean. When I was in college at Texas Tech Univer-

46

sity, I wanted to be a cheerleader so badly. I cheered all through elementary, junior high and high school. It was my life. I had always dreamed of being a college cheerleader, but I didn't have the time to commit during my first few years of college. I didn't try out for the team until right before my senior year. I finally thought, *This is it. Now is my time.* I attended every practice. I took extra gymnastics classes to improve my back handsprings. I also worked on getting in better shape. I did everything I could think of to prepare for these tryouts.

One night before practice, I was in the locker room with a bunch of girls when one of them told me she admired how high my jumps were. She said, "Terri, I love your toe touches. Would you do one for us?" Of course I could. Without stretching or preparing, I jumped up to showcase my signature move. As I was in mid-air, I felt my muscle tear right down the back of my right thigh. When I landed on my feet I crumpled to the ground like a rag doll.

I was devastated. I missed practice that night, which was mandatory. I hurt so much I couldn't even walk to the car on my own. But more than that, I was mad at myself because my torn muscle prevented me from trying out for the cheerleading squad. It was the last shot I had. My injury cost me a dream, and all because I didn't stretch. (Honestly, I don't even know if I would have made it, but I never got the chance to find out.)

Stretching (in more than the physical sense) is what prepares us for going farther than we ever have before. Any time God is getting ready to do something in your life, you will be stretched. In other words, it's going to be uncomfortable. Stretching isn't fun. Nobody likes it. That's why I did the jump without even thinking. But when God is preparing you for something, you're going to have to be flexible and able to bend to His will. That is what ensures you are ready for the move.

47

Let's go back to the quote I shared in the Introduction: "You will never leave where you are until you decide where you'd rather be." I want you to take the time to see beyond today. When you are able to stretch and put thought into what you want, you will realize you are limited only by what you can imagine. What would happen if you were to allow yourself to dream big?

It wasn't until I gave myself permission to dream and actually try my best to see beyond where I was at the moment that I began to see my future, and things started happening to bring my imaginings into reality.

A Map to Know Where You Are Going

When I began writing my dreams down, all of a sudden I knew where I was going. I had a map, and it made a big difference. I want to share something with you that I did a few years ago. On August 22, 2006, I was sitting in my guest bedroom with my laptop, forcing myself to dream. I asked myself, *What is my vision? What do I see in my future?* I have included it here in a sidebar. I didn't want anyone else to see what I had written down (until now, of course); I knew it was between God and me. Sometimes it seems embarrassing to dream or to admit what you see in your heart, but I know there is power in writing the vision down and making it plain.

Personal *Vision*, August 22, 2006

If I'm truly honest with myself, and I think about what's burning in my heart, I know that I see this:

Number one: a television broadcast. I see myself teaching and preaching on my dad's TV show the entire broadcast. I don't know how that would ever happen, but for some reason, I see myself preaching the entire broadcast for a month at a time. I have no idea why. I've never yearned for the spotlight at all. I can't explain it. I just see it. I wonder at times if my dad will call me from overseas or from another state and say, "Why don't you just do the whole broadcast the next couple weeks while I'm gone? When I get back, I'll join you."

Number two: books. Worldwide book distribution. It's humbling to write this type of stuff because I don't want to appear that I'm trying to be famous. That's not it at all. It's just that I'm trying to be as honest as possible about what I see in my future if I obey God and discipline myself to stay focused in pursuing Him. I see my ministry being very successful in book publishing. I see hardback books all over the world. I see them in bookstores. I don't know why I see this, but I truly see it.

Number three: crusades with a theme. It's funny, I don't know what the theme is, but I see a theme threaded throughout the entire conference from beginning to end. I see that so clearly. I see women and teenage girls coming from all over to be a part of those conferences.

Number four: helping troubled teenage girls. I don't know what God wants me to do with this, but perhaps it's because of my past. I see me being involved in helping young girls who are pregnant and don't know what to do. I want to help them cry out to God, see themselves as valuable and continue on with His plan for their lives. I don't know if that means helping people like Mercy Ministries or funding them or speaking to them, but I know I want to help girls who are in trouble.

Number five: a mission in France. I know I didn't study French for no reason. I don't know anyone in France. Don't

49

know what God wants me to do, but I want to be involved in reaching out to the French people. I just trust God's wisdom and His timing in opening doors.

I took the time to listen for God. I'll admit I wasn't confident initially that some of the things I wrote down were from Him. But the more I began to write, the more ideas began to stir on the inside of me. I started to get passionate and desire my dreams more. And I gained more faith that God was, in fact, placing these dreams inside of me.

Five years later, every one of the five things I listed came to pass. In August 2006, I considered them crazy to even think about. In August 2011, they weren't so crazy. They were a reality. God will do the same thing for you. He just needs you to dream and start drawing out your map. And you know what? None of those dreams took five years!

When author Napoleon Hill did a study on the major causes of failure, he found that the lack of a well-defined purpose in life is the biggest reason people don't succeed. There is no hope of success for the person who does not have a definite goal in mind.[5]

My five dreams became a definitive target to shoot toward. They became my life's focus. Although I trusted God's timing in bringing them to pass, I began laying the groundwork for those dreams. For instance, God led me to a publisher, but I had my first book written so that when the publisher wanted to work with me, I was ready. God helped me reach those dreams once I drew my "map." When you have a clear picture and specific details in your mind and on paper, you can begin building toward the life you imagine.

Out of Sight, Out of Mind

I shared the story about Caryl and Marilyn—The Mommies—with my staff one year. At the end of our meeting, I said, "Imagine it's five years from now. How old are you? Where are you? What are you doing? Who are you with?" Then came the big question: "Now tell me, what have you accomplished?" I told them to write down their dreams and, if they were comfortable, share them with me. I wanted to pray over their lists and be in agreement with them. Every one of them did this, and I had the awesome opportunity to read their inspiring dreams.

Six months later, at another staff meeting, I brought up their dream lists. I wanted to see how far along they were in what they wanted to accomplish. I started out by saying, "One of you said you wanted to write four books in the next five years. I'm guessing you are probably about finished with your first book and seeking a publisher or looking into ways to self-publish." I couldn't help but notice the expression on that person's face. Her eyes got really big, and she looked shocked.

I continued, "One of you said you wanted to save $100,000 over the next five years. That means that for the past six months you've probably been saving $1,666.67 every month. Right?" I quickly scanned the room. The person who wrote that down looked at me, his eyes as big as saucers. I am sure he was thinking, *You've got to be kidding me.*

I wasn't trying to call these people out or embarrass them. I wanted to make clear that simply writing down a dream doesn't mean it will happen. You have to keep your dreams in front of you constantly and ask God for guidance to show you how to make these dreams come to pass. (I'll talk more about goal-setting in a later chapter.) You don't want to be shocked months or even years later when you stumble across your dream book and realize, *Oh my goodness! I haven't done one thing to make these dreams come true.*

After I told my staff to write out their five-year plans, I scheduled a meeting with them for a year later. A few days before that meeting, I told them to be ready to update me on their progress. I also asked them to email me their original list so I could view it before we convened.

I love my staff. I think they're the best in the world, and I appreciate every one of these fantastic people. But I knew what was going to happen. Several of them approached me before the staff meeting, and others emailed me with the same request: "Terri, um, do you still have your copy of my five-year dreams? I can't seem to find mine." Turns out that I was right.

Their question spoke volumes. *If they didn't even have a copy of their five-year dream goals,* I mused, *obviously they haven't been keeping their dreams in front of them, which means they're probably not pursuing them.* I even had one person stop me in the hallway and say, "Terri, I can't find my list. I'm not even sure what they are, and I don't really even remember what I wrote." He must not have been serious about those dreams.

I didn't make a spectacle out of the ones who didn't even "pass go," but I was firm in communicating my passion. I want them to be committed to pursuing their dreams. I want them to live on purpose and with purpose. I want them to do the things God is telling them to do.

And I want the same for you!

You are never going to achieve the things you are meant to do if you put your written vision in a drawer and never look at it again, or lose it altogether. It's not until you are determined to keep what you wrote down in front of you that you are going to start building the map to your dreams.

I am happy to report that some staff members made incredible progress. One person wrote, "I want to go to South Africa, New York, Australia, Tanzania and Asia." A year later, that person had already visited South Africa and Tanzania. Another staff member brought a mock-up of the book he wanted to write. He even designed the cover with the title and his photo and told us he'd written 75 percent of the manuscript. He did all of that within one year.

There were other dream-desires that came to pass. One person bought a new home. Another had hardwood floors installed in their house. Several staff members bought cars. Others had opened savings accounts and were saving consistently. A few folks were debt-free, except for their houses. Who saw their dreams come to pass? The ones who wrote their vision down and kept it before their eyes.

I want you to grasp the principle that whatever you focus on will eventually show up in your life. My staff loved the five-year challenge I gave them. They were grateful for the accountability when I told them to email their dreams to me. The assignment helped them stretch their imaginations and what they thought about. Best of all, they loved the results. They loved seeing their dreams become reality. They loved being able to say, "I went on that trip." "I paid off my car." "I sent my children to private school." "I wrote a book." All these things happened because they stayed focused.

A Picture (on Paper and in Your Mind) Is Worth a Thousand Words

I've been reading *The Power of Focus* by Jack Canfield, Mark Victor Hansen and Les Hewitt. They share the story of a woman named Glenna Salsbury who, early in her career, was a single mother with three young daughters. She was weighed down by a house payment, a car payment and a need to rekindle some dreams. Glenna attended a seminar that focused on using your imagination in a vivid way. The speaker pointed out that the mind thinks in pictures, not in words. He said that as we vividly picture what we desire, it would become a reality.

Glenna was moved by this idea. She also knew the biblical truth that the Lord gives us the desires of our hearts (see Ps. 37:4) and that we are what we think (see Prov. 23:7). She was determined to take her written list of desires and turn them into pictures. Glenna arranged these photos in an attractive album and waited expectantly, constantly bringing the images to her mind. The pictures she included in her book were quite specific—a woman in a wedding gown, and a good-looking man in a tuxedo; an island in the sparkling blue Caribbean; college diplomas for her daughters; a female vice president of a company (she wanted to be the first woman vice president of the company where she worked, which at the time had no female officers); and a mortarboard cap representing a master's degree from Fuller Theological Seminary.

Eight weeks later, Glenna was driving down a California freeway. She noticed a beautiful red and white car next to hers. The driver of the car noticed her, too, and smiled. The next thing she knew, the car started following her. As frightened as she was, Glenna finally decided to pull over. Long story short, she met the driver of the car, they fell in love and they got married a few years later.

All of a sudden, more images in her dream album actualized in real life. While they were planning the wedding, Glenna's fiancé told her he had found the perfect place for the honeymoon—St. John's Island in the Caribbean. She kept the dream book a secret until they were moving into a new home, which she had also pictured in the album. There was more. Glenna became vice president of human resources in the company where she worked, completed her master's degree and became one of the first women admitted as a doctoral candidate at Fuller Seminary. Not only did her daughters earn college degrees, but they also created their own photo albums and have seen God at work using this practice. Today, Glenna Salsbury is one of the top professional speakers in the country and a former president of the National Speaker's Association.[6] It sounds like a fairytale, but it is absolutely true.

A key message in *The Power of Focus* is that the more specific the pictures are, the more likely you are to stay focused on them and attract the results you want. Be creative and explore options for reinforcing your vision. Creating a dream book is a great way to start. As the speaker in Glenna's seminar explained, most of us think in pictures, not in words or letters. When I say "blue dress" you don't picture "b-l-u-e" and "d-r-e-s-s." You picture an actual blue-colored dress. When you include pictures in your dream book that represent the desires of your heart, you will stay focused on those imaginings and your desires will begin to grow.

I don't want you to be afraid to dream. As long as you live, there will always be something to experience, something to learn, something to do. There will always be places you need to visit, discover and explore. No one knows what you're capable of doing better than God. You haven't yet met all the people God wants you to meet. You haven't yet seen all that God wants you to see. I believe that you should always be striving toward something, because when you stop striving, you stop . . . period.

So what do you dream of doing? Of being? Of having? Of building? Where do you dream of going? Just as Glenna

55

Salsbury allowed herself to dream, and focused on vivid pictures, you have the same permission to activate your imagination and envision great things. Glenna became a successful person because she saw herself succeeding. She became a wife because she saw herself getting married. She graduated seminary because she saw herself in a cap and gown.

God will give you the desires of your heart. The Bible says so. Get a picture of your dreams. Do the homework and make those images in your mind and in your dream book as vivid and as specific as possible.

You Become What You Behold

I want to brag on my team here at Terri Savelle Foy Ministries. They recently worked hard to surprise me by totally renovating my office at our headquarters in Fort Worth, Texas, while I was on a trip. They painted the walls blue toile, laid hardwood flooring, decorated my bookshelves with my treasured success and motivational books, and creatively decorated my walls with Parisian prints and family portraits—all while I was enjoying a delicious croissant in a patisserie in Paris, France. (Okay, I wasn't there just to indulge in French pastries; I was fulfilling a four-year dream of preaching to thousands of people in the largest church in France.)

During the office renovation, my staff texted me periodically to give me updates on the progress and to send me pictures. One of them asked, "What do you want on the 8' x 17' wall facing your desk?" Without hesitation, I texted back, "Vision! I want a giant vision board!"

When I returned home from France, I could hardly wait to see my beautiful French-themed office and to start creating my future on that large blank corkboard. However, I had so much work to do the first few days back home that I couldn't devote time to the vision board. I was bothered every time I looked up from my desk and saw NOTHING on that wall. No dreams. No goals. No ambition. No vision.

Again, as Proverbs 29:18 tells us, "Where there is no vision . . . the people perish" (*AMP*). With vision, however, we flourish! We come alive. We move from where we are to where we want to be. Whatever we focus our attention on, we attract in our lives. If we focus on nothing, we will attract nothing.

Well, not long after my return, I started hanging pictures of where I see our ministry headed. I had so much fun cutting out images of my vision. Before I knew it, my wall was full of pictures representing the Icing women's conferences, the France ministry, finances, the ministry to teenagers, the ministry to women, our books. Now I love looking up from my desk each day and seeing our future.

What do you see when you look up? A pile of debt? Marriage problems? An overweight body? Bills? A failing career? Hopelessness? Unfulfilled dreams? The Bible tells us, "But we all, with unveiled face, beholding as in a mirror the glory of the Lord, are being transformed into the same image from glory to glory, just as from the Lord, the Spirit" (2 Cor. 3:18, *NASB*). In other words, you become what you behold.

This is a powerful principle. To behold something doesn't mean to glance at it every once in a while. It means a constant, immovable and firm gaze; to look at consistently and constantly. Notice that this Scripture says that we are "transformed into the same image." The same image as what? The image of Jesus, whom we are beholding. What you constantly look at, you become. This is the law of vision.

As mentioned above, Joshua 1:8 and James 1:25 tell us to behold the Word of God. Why? Because what you behold, you

57

become. Joshua 1:8 tells us to behold the Word of God. Why? Because what you behold, you become. What are you beholding? What are you looking at? You need to see images of what your life *can* look like. Stop looking at your life and thinking it's as good as it gets. You have to see something before you can have something.

In Dodie Osteen's book, *Healed of Cancer*, she describes how her body began deteriorating with that disease. When she looked in the mirror, she vividly saw a frail, sick, weak body. She knew she had to change what she *saw* if she was going to get victory over cancer. Dodie went through all her family photo albums and found pictures of when she was in perfect health, alive and full of energy. She hung those pictures up all over the house, on the refrigerator, the bathroom mirror, in picture frames. Dodie needed to see herself healed and alive. She surrounded herself with what "could be" not with what "was." That's vision. That's faith. Today, she is the pictorial definition of health.

You do not have to settle for life the way things are. Make your own dream book or vision board and hang pictures of your financial future, your ideal physical body, your dream vacation, your debt paid in full, your marriage restored, your kids serving God, your business flourishing.

I constantly ask people who attend our conferences, "How many of you don't want to be where you're at today by this time next year?" Every hand goes up, including mine. However, without a clear vision, many people will be exactly where they are today in the years to come.

As I was listening to a CD by Pastor Joel Sims of Jackson, Mississippi, he shared how he told his sweet wife, Peppi, repeatedly (and with great enthusiasm), "We are going to the next level!" She agreeably said, "Great! What does it look like?" What a good question! It was one Pastor Joel had to think about. "What *does* the next level look like?" He began putting images together to answer that question. If you want to go to the next level in your life, you need to see what the next level looks like.

You can be as creative or as simple as you want to be, but do something to surround yourself with images of where you see your life headed. I've covered these principles in this chapter but have summarized them here as a quick guide to help you create a vision board.

Five Steps to Creating a Vision Board

Step 1: Pray and Listen
What is on your mind? What do you feel God is telling you to get serious about pursuing? Is it weight loss? Is it getting debt-free? Is it learning a foreign language? Traveling abroad? Going on a missions trip? Writing a book? Getting your degree? Saving money? Giving to a ministry? What is God speaking to your spirit? Whatever it is, write it down. Make a list of those dreams that are important to you.

Step 2: Find Pictures to Match Your Dreams and Goals
Because we think in pictures (not words), it is very helpful to cut out images that depict your dreams. I have a photo on my vision board of thousands of women at a convention center with the word "Icing" on the backdrop of the stage. That's my vision of where I see my Icing Conferences going. Flip through magazines and tear out images that match your dreams and goals or go online and print out those photos. Write checks in the amount you plan to receive.

Step 3: Purchase a Corkboard, Bulletin Board or Poster Board
Pin or glue all your pictures to the board. You can use a simple poster board available at your local discount department store like Wal-Mart or Target, or jazz it up like I did (I framed a corkboard with an antique frame and painted it to match my office decor. It looks really *chic!*).

Step 4: Be Specific About Your Dream(s)
Habakkuk 2:2 tells us to write the vision and make it plain. You might add your name to a college diploma such as "Terri Savelle Foy—Bachelor of Arts degree." I have a vision board hanging in my laundry room at home on which my whole family has contributed goals. Kassidi has a photo of her dream car with the words "Kassidi's Car" and the price of the car next to it. Type it, write it, or use stencil (I use letters with sequins!).

Step 5: Keep Your Vision Board in Sight
Hang your vision board in a place where you will look at it often. Out of sight is out of mind. The key thought here is to look at it as much as possible. It will force you to be constantly aware of where your life is headed. I like the *Contemporary English Version* translation of Habakkuk 2:2: "I will give you my message in the form of a vision. Write it clearly enough to be read at a glance." The purpose of having a vision board is to keep your vision in front of you.

Don't let this project stress you out if you're not the creative type. Have fun with it. People who have a natural artistic flair will create vision boards that could be sold at an art show; others will create a beautiful mess, but it's just as effective. The board itself isn't as important as what happens to you. It is a tool to give you clarity about what God is speaking

60

to your spirit. You deposit that image on the inside of you and let your faith go to work to produce it.

Do something that will inspire your faith to kick it up a notch. Remember, you can't go to the next level until you see the next level.

God Will Give You Clarity in Seeing Your Dream

The best way to get a clear picture of your dreams is to spend time with God. Imagine if I handed you a bunch of puzzle pieces without the box, without the image of what you're supposed to make, and told you to put the pieces together. You wouldn't even know where to start because you wouldn't know what you're building. Without a picture, without a vision, there's nothing at which to aim, so there's no starting point.

You would spend day after day unsuccessfully trying to put this puzzle together, not having a clue of what the result is supposed to be. What was meant to be a fun game would quickly lose its appeal and become frustrating and boring.

That's exactly the way a lot of us live our lives—busy, but bored and frustrated. We spend a lot of time spinning our wheels, trying to put together a life and create a future, without knowing where we're going. It's like coming to the end of a year and looking back on it thinking, *I know I was busy, but I'm not sure what I did this year*.

Let's turn the tables. If I handed you a puzzle and showed you exactly what to make, wouldn't that be a more exciting challenge? You would see the picture—the big picture—and think, *Okay, it's going to take awhile, but I can do this*. The puzzle may have 2,000 pieces, but it's doable because there is a target in sight. There is a specific vision.

61

The same thing happens when we spend time with God. He begins to make the picture of our dreams clear. He may reveal the image of the puzzle one little section at a time, but eventually the whole image will unfold. And in the process, you won't get bored. You won't get frustrated. You won't feel like throwing the puzzle pieces against the wall and giving up, because you'll be doing something productive. You will be making notable progress toward something that has purpose for you, something that has meaning.

The apostle Paul wrote, "But one thing I do: Forgetting what is behind and straining toward what is ahead, I press on toward the goal to win the prize for which God has called me heavenward in Christ Jesus" (Phil. 3:13-14). Paul knew he had a mark. He had a vision. He had a calling. We need to have the same things.

When I was a young girl, I took gymnastic classes. I remember the first time I attempted a backhand spring. Right before I was going to flip, my coach put his hand on my back and said, "Before you even do it, I want you to close your eyes and visualize yourself doing it." I thought to myself, *Why?* I had been practicing a ton to prepare for this very moment. Coach continued, "I want you to visualize it from beginning to end; visualize taking the first step and visualize landing on your feet." He told me to close my eyes and see myself doing it.

When my husband, Rodney, and I attended a Willie George conference for youth pastors, the auditorium was filled with thousands of leaders. I remember Willie saying, "I want every one of you to close your eyes. I want you to visualize your youth ministry. I want you to imagine what God wants you to do with it." I stood with my eyes closed, trying to picture what God wanted me to do. I had never done anything like that before regarding the ministry. I took a deep breath and started to visualize. I pictured buses of teenagers coming to and filling up our warehouse building. Then I saw hundreds of teenagers coming to the altar to meet Jesus for the first time.

I was so inspired and excited about this new vision. I prayed that God would open doors so we could reach out to more teens in our community. As soon as we returned from the conference, Rodney and I worked with and coordinated new volunteers to help us with the coming growth. We decided to try and get a group of young people who didn't have parents and who had been passed around from shelter to shelter to come to our weekly youth service. It was such a special night, just a couple weeks after the conference, when a bus from the local shelter pulled into the parking lot with a group of those children. That night they packed the altar and asked Jesus into their hearts. I was moved beyond words. I felt overwhelmed because the image that I had conjured up in my spirit was happening right in front of me.

This year, before I traveled to London to preach at a conference, I was praying in my guest bedroom (which by now you've figured out is my dream room and prayer closet). I asked God, "What do You want me to see about this meeting?" As I was still and quiet in His presence, I saw women writing their pains, struggles and heartaches on a piece of paper. They scribbled all the bad stuff that had tormented them for years, whether it was the name of someone who had hurt them or the date of an event that had traumatized them. In my spirit, I saw them bringing that piece of paper to an altar at a church for me to pray over. Then I saw them ripping up the paper. I wrote the vision down because I didn't want to forget it.

I went to London excited to see how God would unfold my vision. I preached one morning and ended the message

63

with this closing, "I want all of you to write your pain on a piece of paper. Then I want you to bring it to tonight's meeting, because tonight we're going to give it a burial." That evening, more than 600 ladies came to the altar, papers in hand. I couldn't stop crying as I watched the women tear them up with much passion and emotion. I marveled at how God had showed me the image of this beautiful purging and healing event before it ever happened, and I couldn't stop thanking and praising Him.

When you spend time with God and open your heart, your mind and your spirit, He will unfold dreams and images before you. He wants you to see what will happen on the inside before you see it happen on the outside. This is an exercise in faith. When we trust the vision He gives us, we will eventually see the evidence in our lives. The dreams He gives you to write down will come to pass.

Your Dream Book Resource Guide

When you are ready to start dreaming, and working toward making those things you envision a reality, the next best step is to make a dream book. I have created one based on the format that I have found works for me. You can either create your own style that works best for you, or you can purchase "My Personal Dreams and Goals Notebook" at my website: www.terri.com.

Here are some other ways to keep your dreams in front of you:

1. Put a bulletin board in your office.
2. Create a scrapbook.
3. Use a photo flip-book.

4. Upload an image to your screen saver on your iPad or laptop.

Whatever format you choose, the important thing is to get images and details about your dreams on paper so that you begin the process of making them real to you. Clip pictures from magazines or print them from an online source. Write out key words in big, bold letters with vivid colors, or create images and text using computer publishing software. Bring out your creative side and allow it to inspire you.

Chapter 3

ASSIGN TIME DAILY TO REVIEW YOUR DREAMS

For as he thinks within himself, so he is.
PROVERBS 23:7, *NASB*

• • • • •

67

• • • • •

How frequently you bring to mind your dreams and keep them in front of you has a huge impact on how they manifest. It is reported that Olympic gold medalist and motivational speaker Bruce Jenner once asked a room full of Olympic hopefuls if they had a list of written goals. Every single person raised a hand. But when he asked how many of them had that list with them right at that moment, only one person could actually produce his list—Dan O'Brien. And it was Dan who went on to win the gold medal in the decathlon in the 1996 Olympics in Atlanta.[1] Believe me, there is great power in writing out your vision and keeping it with you.

This principle sounds a lot like Joshua 1:8 to me. I prefer to read this verse in different translations; it helps to bring a fresh perspective. The *New King James Version* says it this way: "This book of the law should not depart out of your mouth, but you should meditate in it day and night. That you may observe to do all that is written in it, for then you'll make your way prosperous and you'll have good success."

That's God's idea of giving us a success clue. Look at the *New International Version*: "Never stop reading this scroll of the law. Day and night you must think about what it says. Make sure you do everything that's written in it. Then things will go well with you and you'll have good success."

The MESSAGE translation reads: "Don't get off track, either left or right, so as to make sure you get to where you're going. And don't for a minute let this Book of The Revelation be out of your mind. Ponder and meditate on it day and night, making sure you practice everything written in it. Then you'll get where you're going; then you'll succeed. Haven't I commanded you? Strength! Courage! Don't be timid; don't get discouraged. GOD, your God, is with you every step you take."

I love that. God is telling us not to let His Word leave our minds for a minute. We must think on it continually. We can apply that scriptural principle to our vision board by making a daily commitment to keep those dreams and goals in view.

The *A* in *IMAGINE BIG* stands for "assign time daily to review your dreams." Don't ever underestimate the significance of this practice. In this chapter, I will demonstrate how essential it is to keep your dreams always before you so that you don't abandon them. This is similar to how the Bible teaches we should view God's Word. We must study, meditate on and keep it in our hearts and minds at all times so that these powerful words come alive for us. God told the Israelites to literally wear His words on their foreheads and arms (see Deut. 11:18). The ancient people took what God said seriously and wore phylacteries—small boxes that contained verses from the Scriptures. They were never far from His Word in mind, body and spirit.

The same truth applies to our dreams. We must call them to our attention all of the time. Out of sight, out of mind is true. Whether it's an idea, a task or a person, when something or someone is not in front of you, thoughts about them can be completely off your radar. We can't allow our dreams to lie dormant. We have to continue to keep them stirred up by keeping them in front of us.

Seeing What Will Be

I've always been a goal-setter, but not necessarily a goal-getter. In fact, for years I had the habit every January 1 of pulling out a sheet of paper and writing out my big vision for the year. The problem was, I would safely tuck it away in my nightstand and never look at it again. Did I achieve my vision? (Are you kidding me?) A few months later, I couldn't even remember what I had written. In fact, by the end of the year, I didn't even know where I had put that piece of paper. In essence, all I did was give myself the satisfaction of saying that I had written down something, and that's about as far as it went.

There was a consequence for ignoring my vision—my life didn't change. Not one bit. Year after year, I'd write out these grand and purposeful visions and dreams, and then I'd put them somewhere to collect dust. As I look back, I can't believe I wasted all of that time and effort for nothing. My life started changing once I started spending time daily reviewing my dreams. All the things I have imagined in my mind and kept before me are becoming realities. I know that God is the one making them happen, but I am applying the steps He said to take in order to achieve success.

Never in a million years did I want to be a preacher. The whole reason I'm in this ministry is because I am so convinced that God's Word works. It's so exciting! I can't help but want to share that with the world . . . with you. I believe that I am called to inspire the people I encounter through what I have experienced in my own life. And I want to show you that if you'll do what God's Word says to do, you'll have the results that God's Word says you can have. I want you to imagine the possibilities of what you can do with Him. I want you to dream of what you can accomplish. I want you to envision what God has planned for you.

Review these things constantly. Keep them in front of you until you start walking toward them. God is going to give you ideas and new ways of doing things that you never thought of before. He will bring people into your life that will help you accomplish your goals—people you never imagined you would meet, people you only dreamed about meeting one day.

It's necessary to set aside time each day to review, meditate on and pray over your dreams. This morning, when I got back from the gym, I went into my guest bedroom while everyone else was still sleeping. I lifted my dream book up to the Lord and I spoke by faith that every one of my dreams *are* fulfilled. I turned page after page and made those confessions. This is how my dreams are manifesting in my life, by keeping them before me and believing God for them.

The Bible says that we serve a God who speaks of nonexistent things as if they already exist (see Rom. 4:17). He wants us to talk the same talk. Anyone who will dare to put his or her faith into action and believe God to bring forth what seems impossible or unattainable; the one who will go that extra mile and do things that other people think are crazy will realize the fruit of his or her faith.

God is looking for dreamers. He wants you to enlarge your thinking. He wants to think beyond the realm of possibilities. After all, God is the one who will ultimately fulfill these dreams for you. Sure, you'll have to take appropriate steps, but He will open up heaven for you. He will use the unlimited resources He has. He will move mountains. So stop thinking small. God needs you to open your imagination to believe that the dreams you have in your heart can happen for you. Put a demand on your faith to believe for something that's totally impossible, because He specializes in doing the impossible.

I looked up the word "believe" one day. It means to accept as true, genuine or real. You have to accept the fact that God can do anything, because He can. He can do anything with you if you'll just trust Him. Carry these words of truth in your heart, and carry your vision with you. Commit time each day to review your dreams.

W. Clement Stone was a mentor to Jack Canfield before he achieved fame for his *Chicken Soup for the Soul* book. One piece of advice W. Clement Stone gave Jack was to write his most important goal on the back of his business card and carry it in his wallet at all times. Every time Jack opened his wallet, he was reminded of what he had written. It was around this time when his first *Chicken Soup* book was released. Sales figures weren't in yet, but Jack had written on the card, "I am so happy selling 1.5 million copies of *Chicken Soup for the Soul* by December 30, 1994."

Jack's publisher laughed at the absurdity of his goal and told him he was crazy. But by the target date, the book had sold 1.3 million copies. Some might argue he missed his goal by 200,000 copies, and that's true. But the book went on to sell more than 8 million copies in more than 30 languages around the world. Jack may not have hit his target precisely, but that was by no means a failure.[2]

The Power of Change

Let's talk about *your* future. What are you doing with your life? Carefully consider what you do, day in and day out. Now, pretend it's five years from now and you haven't changed anything about your existing habits. You've continued doing the same old same old. If you spend too much money, you're still doing that five years from now. If you watch too much TV, you're still doing that five years from now. If you waste time on Facebook or other social networks, you're doing the same thing five years from now.

What will your life look like in five years? How old will you be? How long have you been at your current job? Where do you live? How much money have you saved? Do you like what you see? That last question can be tough to answer. Years ago, when I asked myself that question, my answer was "No." I didn't like my life. I didn't like what I saw. I didn't like where I was headed—I was headed nowhere. I determined that I didn't want to keep repeating the same things every year. I wanted to grow and have new experiences.

Think about the old adage, "If you keep doing what you've always done, you're going to keep getting what you've always gotten." In order to have more, you must become more. You have to change. You have to put in place new habits, new routines, new practices, new ways of thinking.

Most of us have heard the definition of insanity: repeating the same behaviors but expecting different results. You have got to change what you're doing right now if you want a different future. I want you to imagine a better life. I want you to imagine yourself having, doing and being all the things you dream about. There is no reason you can't change. There is no reason tomorrow can't be better than today.

If you don't like what you're producing and experiencing, then you have to change. You have to change your reactions to circumstances. You have to change your attitude. You have to change your negative thoughts to positive ones. You have to change what you daydream about. You have to change your habits. You have to change what you read. You have to change your friends. You have to change how you talk.

What Do You See?

If you see yourself staying the same, you will. If you see yourself succeeding, you will. John F. Kennedy dreamed of putting a man on the moon. Martin Luther King Jr. dreamed of a country free of prejudice and injustice. Bill Gates dreamed of a world in which every home had a computer connected to the Internet. These life-changers believed that anything is possible. They kept their dreams alive and made a habit of thinking about them constantly. I want you to do the same thing. I want you to assign time daily to review your dreams.

When you take the time to think about your future—to visualize and see the invisible—you are one step closer to making them happen. David Yonggi Cho, founder and senior pastor of the world's largest church congregation, wrote a book about the importance of visualization. In the book, he encourages everyone to create a daily routine of visualizing your future. He believes it's best to do this in the morning, after spending time in prayer. Maybe you are not a morning person and would rather do this in the evening or around lunchtime. That's okay. The most important thing is to do it.

I love the morning, and I use that time to review my dreams. After I pray, I sit quietly on my little chaise lounge, notebook in my lap, and I visualize. I dream. I listen for God's voice. I listen for any inspiration He might give me about my future. Whatever I feel God is speaking to my spirit, I write it down. There is so much power in visualizing your future. It's amazing what God will bring to your mind.

73

Jack Canfield shares in his book *The Success Principles* a story that may change your life the way it did mine. In 1986, he attended a themed party, where invitees were asked to come as they would be in 1991, five years into the future. The partygoers had to stretch their imaginations and create the vision they wanted for their lives and, at this party, act as if it had already come to pass. They were asked to dress the part, talk the part and bring any props that demonstrated their dreams had already come true—books written, awards earned and large paychecks received. The evening was a success. Everyone bragged about their accomplishments, celebrated successes and expressed how happy and fulfilled they were. Then they talked about what was next for them.

Jack went to the party as a best-selling author and brought with him several "reviews" of his number-one *New York Times* bestseller to show people. One man came as a multimillionaire dressed as a beach bum, which was his vision of retirement. Another woman brought a mock edition of *TIME* magazine with her face on the cover. A man who wanted to retire and spend his life as a sculptor showed up in an apron with a hammer and chisel and pictures of sculptures he had made. And so it went all evening long.

Jack explains, "Many of you know this author, Susan Jeffers, who did go on from that transformational evening to publish 17 successful books, including the internationally acclaimed best-selling classic *Feel the Fear and Do It Anyway*. . . . The same thing happened to me. I went on to write, compile and edit over 80 books, including 11 number-one *New York Times* bestsellers. That party where we maintained our future personas for more than four hours, flooded our subconscious minds with powerful images of having already achieved our aspirations. . . . But most importantly, it worked. All of those who attended that party have gone on to realize the dreams they acted out that night and much, much more."[3]

When I first read this account, I was struck when he said the visualization exercise worked and all of the people who attended the party have realized their dreams. I couldn't believe it! What a powerful image! In visualization, the sharper the images are and the more intense you feel, the more likely you are to create the desired result.

Know this: You're not going to create a desired result if you write your dreams down and never look at them again. Success is the result of keeping those images and dreams in front of you, focusing on them, praying over them and thanking God for them. The more time you spend doing this, the more you're going to create a driving desire to go after and ultimately accomplish your dreams.

Wayne State University conducted a study about visualization for athletes using basketball players as their subjects. Half of the players were instructed to lie on the bleachers every day and visualize themselves shooting free throws. The other half of the team did their daily free throw shooting drills without visualizing. Both groups shot free throws consistently, and both groups improved their skills. However, the squad that spent time visualizing before shooting actually saw their averages rise much higher than those who didn't. It's amazing what visualizing can do.[4]

Most of the world's greatest achievers visualize their dreams. Some of them have dream walls, dream boards or dream books, and they are very specific about what they want to accomplish over the next year, the next 5 years, 10 years, or more. Every successful person I know, and every successful person I have studied, does this in some fashion. They visualize.

75

They imagine. They see themselves succeeding before they succeed. They keep their dream before them.

What are some of the dreams you had when you were a child? What about when you became an adult? Are you living the life you imagined? If not, why not? What is stopping you? What is holding you back? Why can't you go back and get that college degree? Why can't you write that book? Why can't you learn to speak a foreign language? Why can't you travel to Africa? Why can't you volunteer overseas?

If you consider the possibility of making your dreams become a reality and take appropriate steps toward them, your life could be different in five years. You could be taking those flying lessons, learning a new skill, mastering a musical instrument, or have started a youth ministry. I believe that if you can conceive it in your mind, you will receive it in your life. Make a commitment to your future and assign daily time to review your dreams.

Quotable Quotes

You can have excuses or you can have results,
but you're not going to have both.
UNKNOWN

You only have control over three things in your life. Number one, the
thoughts you think. Number two, the images you visualize. And
number three, the actions you take. . . . How you use these three
things determines everything you experience.
JACK CANFIELD, *NEW YORK TIMES* BESTSELLING AUTHOR

Always dream big dreams. Big dreams attract big people.
DAVID LINIGER, CEO OF REMAX

It doesn't create any more energy to create a big dream than it does to create a little one.
GENERAL WESLEY CLARK, U.S. ARMY (RET.)

Your brain can achieve a lot more when you effectively use the power of visualization.
DAVE MARTIN, SUCCESS COACH

Thinking is the hardest work there is, which is probably the reason so few engage in it.
HENRY FORD, AMERICAN INDUSTRIALIST

The secret to getting ahead is getting started. The secret of getting started is breaking your complex, overwhelming task into small manageable tasks and then starting on the first one.
MARK TWAIN, AUTHOR

If you want to see change in your life, change something you do daily.
JOHN MAXWELL, *NEW YORK TIMES* BESTSELLING AUTHOR AND LEADERSHIP EXPERT

The person who stops studying merely because they finished school is hopelessly doomed to mediocrity no matter what their calling.
NAPOLEON HILL, BESTSELLING AUTHOR

A winner knows how much he still has to learn, even when he's considered an expert by others. A loser wants to be considered an expert by others before he has learned enough to know how little he knows.
SYDNEY HARRIS, JOURNALIST

77

Everything starts in your mind. The thoughts you have about yourself will make you or break you. You are what you think, and you will attract the images that dominate your mind. If you see yourself as poor, you'll stay poor. If you see yourself as lonely, you'll stay lonely. If you see yourself as barely surviving, you'll barely survive. If you see yourself as receiving that promotion, you'll be promoted. Your life is constantly moving toward the dominating images in your mind.

As I explained in chapter 2, when I wrote down some dreams back in 2006, they were big dreams that didn't make sense or fit with the way my life looked at the time. Five years later, my life had shifted dramatically to incorporate those dreams. I believe it's because I kept those images in front of me day and night.

What are you looking at? What are you thinking about? Where is your focus? Is your attention directed toward success or failure? The answers are up to you. According to Romans 8:37, you are more than a conqueror. You are capable of doing anything you set your mind to as long as God is on your side.

Make It a Habit

You can change the course of your life in just five minutes a day. If you were to set aside that time to simply think, visualize and imagine your life in the future, it could open up a whole new world of opportunities, relationships, resources and ideas that you never thought possible. I want to challenge you to make this a habit. Discipline yourself. Go somewhere every day this week for five minutes. It can be in the morning or whenever your schedule allows. Just sit quietly and think. Be still.

My life didn't change much until I began taking the time to visualize my future, to consider what God wanted me to do. Once I opened myself up to that thought process and to His leading, He did more in my life in five years than in the 15 years prior to that. Why? Because I made myself start a habit of spending just five minutes a day without distractions, allowing my mind to explore ideas and receive the messages God had for me.

The best way to start a habit is to do it the same time every day. It's hard to be consistent without a routine. It's like taking vitamins or drinking coffee or any other habitual action. You probably take your vitamins or drink your coffee at the same time every morning. You don't have to think about it. You don't have to remind yourself to do it. You just do it.

Visualizing and reviewing your dreams and your vision can be done the same way. Make it a habit, a routine. Maybe there is a best time for you: before you go to work, before you go to school, during lunchtime or after the kids go to bed. At first, you may have to force yourself to have some private time with God. Soon enough, it will become second nature.

As you sit quietly and visualize, pray over your dreams. Look at each one of them, see them as already achieved and praise God as if they've already happened. I fit this time into my routine before I even get dressed and ready for the day. I know that if I wait until after I'm dressed for the office, it never works out. Something inevitably goes wrong, and I run out of time. Either my hair looks crazy that day and I have to spend extra time on it, or I have to keep applying more mascara. But, if I put this time into practice at the beginning of my day, everything else falls into place.

Here's the thing: The less time you spend keeping your dreams in front of you, the less motivated you will be to go after them and the more impossible it will seem to make them become reality. But when you're reviewing your dreams constantly,

79

you can see yourself achieving them. I want you to figure out the best time for you to visualize and review your dreams. Commit to doing this daily review for the next 21 days, until it becomes part of your daily routine and you don't have to think about it. It is said that it takes three weeks to make or break a habit, so give yourself this 21-day challenge to develop the habit of making time to review your dreams. Once you have mastered this, you can apply this principle to any other area of your life where you need to start good new habits or break bad old ones.

I recently read a story about bestselling fiction author Debbie Macomber. When she decided to pursue her dream of becoming a writer, she rented a typewriter and kept it on the kitchen counter. She would type each morning after her kids left for school and then again after they went to bed. One night, her husband sat her down and explained that money was tight. They were barely getting by on his income alone and couldn't continue that way much longer. Debbie was heartbroken. She knew that having a full-time job on top of keeping up with the many responsibilities of maintaining a house, caring for the kids and managing all their activities would leave her no time to write.

The next morning, her husband sensed her despair and asked what was wrong. Debbie told him she believed she could make it as a writer. He agreed to find a way to help her pursue her dream, and Debbie eventually returned to her writing. While she pressed on, the family scrimped and saved everywhere they could—forgoing vacations, pinching pennies and wearing hand-me-downs. After five years of financial struggle, Debbie's persistence and sacrifice paid off, and she sold her first book. Today, Debbie has published more than 100 novels, many of which are *New York Times* bestsellers, and three that have been made into movies.[5]

Here is what I admire about Debbie. To accomplish her dreams, she established a routine. She got up every morning at the same time. She then read her Bible, wrote in her journal, got in some exercise and responded to emails. Then she sat down at the typewriter. She diligently wrote during the block of time she had without her kids at home and was able to produce three new books a year with this system of discipline. Let me say it again: The secret of your future is hidden in your daily routine.

Build Your Faith

Are you having a hard time reviewing and keeping your dreams in front of you? I don't want anything to stop you from doing what God is nudging you to do. I don't want you to give up. I think some people believe that we should only pray for the things we believe are actually possible. But isn't that limiting God? It's critical to trust Him for everything, including the dreams and the vision we can't fully conceive.

When you are challenged to dream, build your faith. Why? Because it will take faith to override the fear that may be keeping you from realizing those dreams. Fear comes from all different directions. You may fear that you'll never change. You may fear that your spouse will leave you. You may fear foreclosure on your house. You may fear that you will never lose weight. You may fear staying stuck. You may even fear success. All of our fears stand in the way of believing in God and believing for success. We will explore some ways to build faith in later chapters, but I want you to be mindful of the fact that fear keeps you in bondage to attitudes, behaviors and habits that limit dreams or vision.

A friend of mine, Martine Wilkie, wrote a book called *Be Thin, Be Free*. In it she writes, "Free and thin people don't think,

81

'I'll gain weight if I eat this cake. It's 12 o'clock, I must eat lunch. I must eat everything on my plate. I know I'll gain weight if I eat those carbs.'"[6] She explains that the reason is because free and thin people don't think constantly about food and weight. Maybe you've struggled with weight your whole life. It's time to start a new routine and develop right thinking. You can overcome your fear of gaining weight or your fear of never losing weight by building your faith. Remember, the more faith you have, the less fear you have.

Little Changes Count

Your life will never change until your routine changes. I call my magazine *The Routine* because I am convinced that (pardon the repetition) the secret of your future is hidden in your daily routine and how you go about living day to day. You don't lose weight or get in shape by doing one grueling three-hour workout. Change happens by doing something small, over and over again, like walking 15 minutes a day, six days a week.

Unless you've won the lottery, depositing one check into your savings account will not financially secure your future; but routing a regular and consistent portion of your paycheck to that account will build toward a solid financial future.

One long prayer time on your knees is not what will change your life. Change comes through daily appointments with God, sometimes for 5 minutes, sometimes for 10, sometimes for 30. The amount of time isn't as important as consistently connecting with and loving on God, and staying aligned with His will. It's not just one moment that's going to change your life; it's the discipline of developing a habit—a routine—that will bring about the most impact.

I want to encourage you to set a goal to build your faith daily. You might think you don't have time. I disagree. I know you have time. You have time while you're getting ready for the day, while you're driving, while you're cooking, while you're doing laundry, while you're waiting for your child at the school pick-up, while you're taking a bath, while you're taking a walk, while you're on the elliptical machine at the gym. You have time to build yourself up on a daily basis, to challenge your faith and to pursue your dreams. If you want to see change in your life, change something you do daily.

Sometimes the biggest life goals seem overwhelming; but when you set measurable goals with reasonable deadlines, and determine the actions you need to take (I'll talk about that in the next chapter), all of a sudden they seem much more manageable. Instead of making one major, drastic change, I want you to focus on changing a little at a time.

Years ago, my husband and I began saving loose change in a jar. Rodney would empty his pockets at the end of the day, and I would clean out my wallet a little at a time. It was a few pennies here, a little silver there. Months went by, and it looked like we might have accumulated about $7 at that point, but we continued our routine. One day, when I was pregnant with Kassidi, we got our first bill from the obstetrician. The doctor's charges came to $348. We had no idea how we would pay it, because we had no extra money. Suddenly, it dawned on us that we had the change jar. Maybe it would make a dent in the bill.

My husband and I took the change to the bank to see how much we had saved. Just for fun, I made a wild guess at the amount, and I challenged Rodney to do the same. We each wrote down our guesses. Mine was $78. Rodney thought it was $92. We watched as the bank teller poured the pennies, nickels, dimes and quarters into a giant bin that instantly calculated the amount. Would you believe that we had $372 in

• • • • •

83

• • • • •

change? Twenty minutes earlier, we were worried about where we would get the money to pay the medical bill, and we ended up having more than enough!

The principle that little bits of change add up to a lot of money, little by little, applies to every area of your life. Every bit of change you make builds on previous changes and becomes something greater than you imagined. You may not think that getting up five minutes earlier every day to build your faith will have any impact. But when you use that time by going to a quiet, private room and spending time with God, it is going to make a big difference. It's not the amount of time you spend with Him that changes your life. It's the fact that every day you are choosing to spend time with Him. This act proves that you are committed to obeying God and living for Him.

Are you still frightened by the prospect of dreaming big things? Are you building your faith? Are you consistent about it? Start by setting a goal to spend 5 minutes with God every day. One day you may want to spend 10 minutes with Him because you have more on your mind or because you realize you are getting so much out of it. If you are not constantly looking at your watch but are reading His Word, praying and listening for His voice, you will hear what He has to say and discover incredible things. All of a sudden, you will find yourself enjoying this time and desiring to spend even more time with Him. You will discover that this goal is more than a routine part of your day. It becomes the most essential element, because it affects your attitude and your outlook in so many positive ways.

With each time you spend communing with the Lord, the bits of healing, insight and joy you receive add up. It brings about change in your life. It renews your mind. It brings you joy. It brings about big dreams. Soon you will realize your faith is a whole lot stronger ever since you started spending five minutes a day with God.

Little changes add up. Whether it's working out, saving money, building a relationship or increasing your faith—every bit matters.

Knowledge Is the Key to the Kingdom

Another way to keep your dream in front of you is to continually learn. Successful people never stop acquiring knowledge in the field related to their purpose. They never assume they know everything. They understand that learning is a lifelong process. We have a tendency to feel overwhelmed when we think of everything we are "supposed" to know or everything we have yet to learn. But if we knew everything, guess what? We would stop living. This is another area where it's critical to take baby steps and make little changes.

Figure out what you need to learn to achieve your dream, and make a list of the resources you can use to do it. Take the first step and purchase a book that you believe is going to help you renew your mind, stretch your thinking and expand your vision. Choose a book that will inspire you to grow and reach your dreams. The next step is to schedule a time to begin reading it. If you can dedicate even 20 minutes a day, it might take awhile to finish the book, but you would steadily make progress and eventually finish it. At the end of the month, that's 10 hours dedicated to learning.

Recently, I decided to allot 30 minutes a day when I got home from work to reading that I believed would help me pursue and keep my dreams in front me. That's all I committed to—30 minutes. Sometimes on the weekends, especially on Saturday mornings, I would read for a longer period of time

· · · · ·

85

· · · · ·

than my assigned goal—sometimes for an hour, and maybe even for an hour and a half. Before I realized it, a month had passed and I had read three books.

You may be shaking your head and saying, "But, Terri, I don't have time to read. I have young kids. I have a full-time job. I have to care for my elderly parents." I get it. I understand that most of us lead busy lives and are trying to get by while juggling a handful of tasks and responsibilities. But I also know that it is possible to find time. Sometimes you have to be a little creative or sacrifice certain habits that may not be the best use of your time. Look at it this way: If you can cut out 30 minutes of TV time each day and devote that time to reading, it will make a difference in maintaining your vision.

On another note, you may feel that you can't commit to reading something that will help catapult your dreams because it will take precious time away from your family. Here's what I've learned. It can actually be the best thing you can do for your family, because you are helping yourself to grow; and when you grow, you become a better individual. When you become a better individual, you are a better influence on your family.

I reached my goal of reading regularly in small increments, and it didn't negatively affect my relationship with my daughter or my husband. Kassidi and I are always together, but it didn't faze her when I said, "I'm going to go in the other room and read for a bit." She would hang out by herself and do her own thing during this time. When I was done, I was ready to spend time with her and Rodney, and I felt empowered, refreshed and energized.

Assign a time to review your dreams by educating yourself. Don't ever get the idea that school's over. Just because you aren't working on a degree is no reason to stop trying to build and expand your knowledge. Every successful person I know, have met or have observed has one thing in common: They are constantly reading. They are constantly educating themselves. If you don't like to read, then download audio books to your iPod or your iPhone, or get books on CD to listen to while you drive, while you work out or while you clean the house. Do whatever you need to do to keep learning, growing and gaining knowledge.

I require my staff to read leadership books. We read a few chapters a week, then meet to discuss what we've read. I challenge them in this way so that our team is always growing and learning new things. I don't want us to get comfortable where we are. I want us to stretch ourselves to do more, learn more, and be more. Your success will only grow to the extent that you grow. Luke 12:48 tells us that to whom much is given, much is required. I like how Bill Chandler, entrepreneur and founder of Mental Wealth, rephrases this truth: "Much is required in order for much to be given."

If you're always on the go, listen to motivational messages as you drive (it's like going to college in your car). Listen to (or read) inspiring books that stretch your mind—your thoughts and beliefs. Set a goal to read a certain number of books this year. Imagine how much more knowledgeable you'll be at the end of the year. Remember, when you're through changing, you're through.

If the dream God has given you is to be financially secure when you retire, consider buying the book *The Automatic Millionaire* by David Bach. Designate a block of time on your schedule—maybe every night before you go to bed, or the first thing in the morning when you have your coffee—and, no matter what, spend that time reading the book. Do some research and find a workshop, conference or class that has to do with

87

your particular dream, and attend that event. You could also make a phone call to your bank or to a financial advisor and set up an appointment to talk about your goals. Make yourself do it. Learn from others. Chances are that somebody has already done what you want to do and you can glean wisdom and guidance from their expertise.

There is a certain species of fish that grows according to its environment. If you place that tiny fish in a small container, it will remain small. If you place that same fish in a large body of water, it will grow to its intended size. People are the same way. If you remain in an environment that doesn't challenge you or promote growth, you will stay small. However, if you get around "big fish" and people who imagine big, you will grow to your God-intended size.

For example, if your dream is to make more money, you have to spend time with people who are making salaries you dream of earning. Studies reflect that we typically make within a few thousand dollars of the average of the five people we most hang around. I call that a comfort zone. Sure, it can be intimidating and uncomfortable to hang out with millionaires, but that is what you need to do to realize your dream.

The fact is, when you feel stretched and out of place, it means that you are growing. Hang out with people who think bigger than you do. Hang out with people you can learn from. Hang out with people who build you up and challenge you. Don't just hang out with people who make you look smart; hang out with those who help you grow.

What Are You Doing?

What you do on a daily basis leads you to either success or failure. One of the most powerful goals for high achievers is that they plan their day the night before. They spend a few minutes at the end of each day making a To-Do list.

I'm a planner at heart, so this comes naturally to me. I enjoy it. I like mapping out my day ahead of time and being able to look at it laid out so that I know what to expect. I use my calendar to list everything I need to get done. This is helpful for keeping me focused throughout the day. I feel that I accomplish more because I have a guide for the tasks that need my attention. Instead of giving in to the attitude "whatever happens today happens," and letting interruptions control me, I can move through my day with purpose and direction.

You're not going to pursue your dreams by wandering aimlessly. You have to be in control of your day. You have to be in control of your time. You have to be in control of your activities. Take a closer look at how you spend your day. Develop a routine. Make a schedule and stick to it. I read some statistics the other day that reported that the average American adult (18 years and older) watches almost six hours of TV a day. Six hours! If you were to cut out even one hour of TV a night, you would gain 30 hours a month of extra time. That's more than a day![7] One hour may not seem like a lot, but when you look at how that affects a month's worth of your time, it looks a whole lot different.

What would you do with 30 extra hours a month? Would you read? Exercise? What else? Use your time wisely. You have more time than you realize. Use it to keep your dreams in front of you. Use it to learn. Use it to make small changes that result in big dividends. It won't take long to see the positive impact of choosing to do things that take you closer to achieving your dream. And your life will begin to change in tremendous ways.

When you expand your mind, you are already taking steps to realize your dream. Spending time each day reviewing your

89

dreams becomes a thrilling and active practice when you are not only envisioning what you want to do, but you are also taking the right measures to make those dreams happen. In the next chapter, you will learn about tools to take your dreams out of your head and off the paper. We will begin putting them into motion so that they are able to take shape and grow.

Making a Schedule Map

A schedule map is a tool I use to keep myself on track. It allows me to manage my daily life responsibilities while incorporating time to pursue my dreams.

90

1. Get Yourself a Month-at-a Glance Calendar

You need to see the big picture. Each day has specific things that must be done, but it's easy to get bogged down in those little things and forget to make time for the big stuff, like pursuing your dreams. Build time into your schedule each week to take on at least one goal that is a building block for your dream. Sometimes it might even be necessary to let a household chore sit an extra day, or delegate it to someone else so that you are giving yourself time for this important part of your life.

2. Plan Your Day the Night Before

Sit down with your calendar and your To-Do list each night before bed and organize your tasks for the day. See what errands you can clump together, and map out the route so you aren't repeatedly going from one side of the city to the other. If you can make a loop, starting at home and working your way around to each location until you've arrived back at home, then you will make much better use of your time.

3. Group Like Tasks Together

One way to continue spinning your wheels, getting nowhere, is to jump from one thing to another without any direction or purpose. If you have housecleaning, computer work and errands on your To-Do list for the day, don't try to do all of them in the same block of time. Errands require being away from home and a certain kind of focus. Household chores are physically demanding. Computer work is mentally taxing. So don't try to do laundry while you are paying the bills or responding to email. The up and down, back and forth is distracting, and you will spend more time trying to figure out where you were than if you had stayed at your desk and completed that task before moving on to washing clothes.

4. Stay Encouraged

If you have a day where you can't get to a single thing on your list because of unexpected interruptions, don't let this derail you. Don't become discouraged or disappointed in your progress. This is what happens in life. You can't schedule everything. But this is also why it's essential to map out your day the night before. Sit down with your list and see what you have for the next day and where you can shuffle things around to take care of what wasn't done today. This will also force you to look at what really has to be done and what can be eliminated. If you are trying to fill your limited time with too many things, you may need to consider where you can say no or where you can turn a responsibility over to someone who is waiting in the wings to help you.

91

Chapter 4

Get goals in place

Where there are no goals, neither will there be significant accomplishments; there will only be existence.
ANONYMOUS

So far, we've gone through the reasons we need to dream and have explored ways to do that. We've covered the value of spending daily time reviewing our dreams and keeping them with us. We know that our dreams become visions when we partner with God to accomplish the things He put us here to do, and that sometimes it requires the faith to move mountains. Now we are going to climb those mountains that can feel overwhelming. God doesn't want us to back away from our dreams because they look too big. I'm going to share with you how to shrink them down to something you can manage and accomplish.

One of the most critical elements of success is setting goals. You can't imagine big things for your life and not set personal goals to help those imaginings come to pass. This chapter will offer tips for setting personal goals that aim toward bringing life to your dreams. I've learned from personal experience that success doesn't happen without a plan. People who tap into the potential God gave them do so because they set personal goals for themselves and stick to them.

Someone once said that without a goal, it's difficult to score. That's a good point. Why play a game if you don't have a goal? You are a player in the game of life. God has a unique plan just for you; but it won't happen if you sit around and just wish for it. You have to prepare for it.

The *G* in *IMAGINE BIG* stands for "get goals in place." Setting goals gives you a reason to get up and do what you have to do. Every year I used to set the same New Year's resolution of "getting closer to God." The problem was, I never determined exactly how I would go about doing that. Consequently, nothing changed. It's the same kind of thing to say, "I want to lose weight this year," but never figuring out exactly how much weight you want to lose, by what date, the kind of diet and exercise plan you are going to use, and when you're going to get started. Ambitions are great, but you have to begin with some idea of how to achieve them. Nothing you imagine will happen if you neglect to nail down the particulars. As we move forward, I will provide strategic steps for setting goals that will stretch you and bring you up to a new level.

Set Specific Goals

Diana Scharf Hunt, an American author and time-management guru, said, "Goals are dreams with deadlines." Andrew Carnegie said, "If you want to be happy, set a goal that commands your thoughts, liberates your energy, and inspires your hopes." I also learned from Jack Canfield, who said, "In order to make a goal effective, it needs to answer two questions. How much and by when?"[1] Each of these individuals has realized great success because they were specific in what they wanted, how they wanted it, why they wanted it, and when they wanted it.

It's not enough to say, "I dream of writing a book one day," or "I would like to be thinner," or "I want to be successful." You need the details. You have to know exactly where you are going so that you know how to get there. For example, you could say, "I want to lose 15 pounds," but that's not as effective as saying, "I will weigh 110 pounds by March 15, at 10:00 AM." Habakkuk 2:2 doesn't just say we need to write down the vision; it says we must also "make it plain."

If your dream is to write a book, create the title of your book and figure out when you want to complete it. Then determine how many pages you have to write each day to meet that deadline. If you want to lose weight, decide how many pounds you will lose and what method will be most successful for your lifestyle and goals; then set a target date and begin changing your habits. Whatever your dream, calculate how many dollars you need, how many square feet it will take, how many miles you have to go, how much schooling it will require, or what research you need to do.

Most people hate deadlines. They hate the pressure and the anxiety of something hanging over their head. But without deadlines, nothing would ever get done. The truth is, deadlines are only stressful for procrastinators, those people who aren't diligently working toward meeting them. Put a target date on your dreams and you will find that you are far less likely to let a day go by without reviewing your dream book and taking appropriate steps to reach your dreams.

Remember this: *Vague goals produce vague results.*[2] Don't say, "I want to be successful," because every person has a different definition of what successful means. Be specific about what success is to you. Does it mean retiring at the age of 50? Having a big family? Becoming a CEO of a company? Creating your own company? Be clear about what you want and what it takes to get it. You probably have heard the saying, "Be careful what you wish for, you just might get it." If you aren't specific about what you want, and you don't have a detailed plan for it, you could end up with something that doesn't even resemble your dream.

Measure Twice, Cut Once

There is a difference between having a good idea and having a goal. A goal is clear-cut; a good idea is usually vague. A good idea would be something like the following: *I would like to own a nice home by the ocean.* You might think that is specific, but a "nice home" for you might be a three-bedroom bungalow, whereas someone else might consider a nice home a 20-room mansion. "By the ocean" could mean on the coast of Florida, California or maybe even the South Pacific. A specific goal is: *I will own a 4,000-square foot home on the Pacific Coast Highway in Malibu, California, by noon on April 30, 2014.*

Another attribute of a specific goal is to make a declarative statement. Instead of saying, "I *want* to lose weight," you have to be more confident in your commitment to your goal and say, "I *will* weigh 110 pounds." when you outline your dreams as specifically as possible, and in the form of positive affirmations, and then you chart a detailed course for turning them into realities, you'll be amazed at all you can achieve.

Who do you think God is going to bless? The person who knows exactly what she wants and why she wants it, or the person who says, "Oh, Lord, whatever. You know, just take care of my situation. I need a lot of money. Increase my life, God. In Jesus' name, I'm going to increase." Hmmm. I like the boldness with which that prayer ended, but "increase" what? Your waistline? Your family? Your household budget? What do you believe will increase? Remember: What you understand a term to mean could be quite different from how someone else interprets it. Declare exactly what it is that you're believing God for, and be as detailed as possible. Imagine how much more God wants to bless us when we ask Him for specific things.

When we are precise in our prayer, and God meets that particular need, we know without a doubt that God made it possible. There is no question that it is God who is blessing us and who deserves the praise. Here's another thing to consider: If you are ambiguous in your dreams, how are you ever going to know when you've got what you wanted?

I am challenging you to create a detailed list of what's involved in achieving your goals. We read in Luke 14:28, "Won't you first sit down and estimate the cost to see if you have enough money to complete it?" Why would you take on any task without knowing what you were getting yourself into?

In chapter 3, I mentioned something that is worth repeating: *One of the common characteristics of successful people is that they plan their day the night before.* It allows them to know what they are facing the next day. They are aware of what is on their agenda and can prepare for it. They aren't wasting time each morning trying to organize their thoughts, tasks and responsibilities. They already know what is in store and they hit the ground running. I heard someone say, "Today's preparation determines tomorrow's achievement." By using this same practice when you begin preparing for your dreams—the vision God has given you—you are going to do amazing things.

Recently, I was praying about a financial concern. I sat in a hotel room in Jonesville, Arkansas, and I was stretching my faith by asking God for a specific support contribution for my ministry. I was declaring out loud, over and over, "Lord, I thank You for millions of dollars!" Finally, I stopped. When I quieted down, I felt the Lord, in His loving way, ask me, "For what? What do you need millions of dollars for?" I felt socked between the eyes, because the truth was, I couldn't answer His question with a thorough plan. I chose a random amount of money that, in my mind, sounded good.

It made me think about Kassidi. If she were to ask me, "Momma, can I have a hundred dollars?" my immediate response would be, "Why do you need a hundred dollars? What is it for?" But, if she said, "I need a hundred dollars for volleyball. My shoes cost $60, volleyball camp is $25, and lunch with the team is $15," that's another story. Since she demonstrated her need for the money and outlined a plan of how it would be spent, of course I would give her a hundred dollars. But, to walk up and ask for a significant amount of money without an explanation of how it will be used, to me, is unreasonable.

It works the same way with God. God doesn't hand out blessings without expecting us to offer an accounting of how we have used them. "From everyone who has been given much, much will be required" (Luke 12:48, *NASB*). So when you ask Him for something, be prepared to explain why you need it and how you will use it. Be prepared to give Him a plan.

This is another reason it's crucial to be specific about your dreams and your goals. Know what you're facing, what's involved in getting there, and how you need to prepare. If you want to finish that higher-learning degree, how much is college tuition? Research it and write it down.

How much is your dream vacation? Do the homework. How much is the airplane flight? The hotel? The excursions?

How much money will it take to start a charity for the homeless in your community? Who do you need to talk to on the township board?

Terri Savelle Foy • www.terri.com

In other words, *get prepared*. My dad always says, "My faith doesn't work on approximates. It works on exacts. Don't say we need about $5,000 if we really need $5,432.77. If you ask for $5,000, and that's what you are given, what can you really say when you come up $432.77 short? After all, you were given what you asked for."

I was reading a book by Napoleon Hill called *Think and Grow Rich!* In it he teaches five principles for creating wealth. They have to do with being specific in your plan of action.

- Determine the exact amount of money you desire.
- Set a definite date.
- Make a detailed plan and begin at once.
- Write out a clear and concise statement about the amount you desire.
- Read your written statement aloud twice a day.[3]

99

Know exactly what you are believing God for. Write your vision and make it plain. Speak as if it already exists. Act as if it already exists. And rejoice as if it already exists.

Create S.M.A.R.T. Goals

Many times when people set goals they write them out in a moment of inspiration, but don't review them on a regular basis (or ever). I was like that. I would set my New Year's goals, but within a matter of days I couldn't even find the list I had made. Once I intentionally started reviewing my goals daily and speaking the desired results with my own mouth, I discovered that I was much more successful at accomplishing them. Now they are never out of my sight.

Tricks of the Trade

Setting goals is a great tool for realizing your dreams. Sometimes the first step is to master smaller tasks that weigh you down so you can focus on your dreams. Maybe one of the things standing in your way is a messy house. Maybe it needs some major cleaning. Maybe the amount of chaos and clutter in your life makes you feel like it's impossible to dream. One way to move past these obstacles is to treat them as goals rather than chores.

Here are some tips for mastering your tasks and responsibilities to make the most of every day:

1. *Identify Your Goal*—If your goal for the day is to complete household chores, begin by focusing on a single room.

2. *Break Down the Goal into Manageable Parts*—Make a To-Do list of tasks, and be specific about what you want to achieve.

3. *Set a Schedule*—Determine how long you'd like to spend on each component of the task. Work diligently to stick to it, and adjust in other areas, if necessary, to stay on track.

4. *Check Off Completed Tasks*—Mark off what you've completed from your list as you go so you have a picture of the progress you are making.

5. *Evaluate Your Work*—Look at what you've finished and assess where you might have gotten distracted or in what environment you did your best work.

These insights will be useful as you move on to the next goal.

6. *Plan Ahead*—While you are on a roll and feeling successful, sit down and map out your next goal. Use the momentum as motivation for moving forward. Stay excited and energized.

Whatever your goal is, keeping the big picture in front of you helps you see where you are going. The details keep you from feeling overwhelmed or getting sidetracked.

I keep a fairly detailed calendar and always put the big goals for the month at the top with a target due date next to each goal. Then I fill in the calendar with the daily stuff. It helps to keep the vision in front of me and makes it easy to review every day. It's been said that goals that are not written down are just wishes. Don't let your dreams sit idle because you haven't written them down and laid out a plan for making them happen.

101

A popular acronym used for goal setting is "S.M.A.R.T." which means:

Specific
Measurable
Attainable
Realistic
Timely

I'll unpack these descriptions and we will explore some of them in detail in the sections that follow.

Specific

A specific goal has a much greater chance of getting accomplished than a general goal. When you have a clear picture of what you want to achieve, you have a leg up on the challenge. You know where to start. You can see out in front of you to know where you are headed. You can anticipate obstacles and plan for working around them. You won't get detoured by roadblocks. Finally, you are keeping the finish line always in sight, and that's what keeps you motivated.

Measurable

A measurable goal is what allows you to calculate the cost, prepare for what's required and track your progress. Measuring isn't just counting how many days until your deadline or how many dollars you need before you reach your target. It's a means for you to know how you are advancing toward your dream.

Attainable

Attainability is critical to success. Be sure that you can reach your goals. Don't set yourself up for failure or doom yourself to disappointment before you even get started. Aspiring to find employment as an astrophysicist is great as long as you recognize that you don't walk in off the streets without any education or training to acquire that job. It requires years of schooling and a knack for science. You have to prepare for your dream with the proper steps.

Realistic

When setting goals, they must represent an objective that is not only attainable but also realistic. It's okay to dream big and shoot for the stars, but you have to properly decide how high your goal should be. If your goal is to lose weight, dropping

100 pounds by swimsuit season when you've just made the decision to start in March is not only an unrealistic goal, but it is also unsafe. Even though we trust God to make a way and we believe in miracles, we still must set goals that work within our best interests.

Timely

When there is no timeframe attached to your goal, there is no sense of urgency. If you don't make an effort to schedule time for your dreams, they will take a backseat to all the other demands of life. They will easily fall by the wayside. You'll find yourself five years down the road and no closer to your dreams. In fact, if you aren't progressing, you are regressing, because nothing in life is stationary. Keep that in mind. You are either moving forward or backward. Which direction do you want to go?

103

Set a Deadline

We touched on the importance of scheduling time to go after your dreams and for fulfilling the goals you set for them. Let's look at that in a little more depth. You have to set a time to do something, or it will not happen. How many times have you said to a friend, "Let's get together for dinner or go out for lunch sometime," only to forget what you said five minutes later and go on with life until the next time your paths cross and you say the same thing all over again?

Rodney and I see a particular couple every Sunday at church. Each week we say how we need to get together, but we never actually plan for it to happen. Before we realize it, months have gone by and we still have not gotten together. The truth is, Rodney and I will never hang out with that couple until one of us takes the initiative to say, "Okay, next Sunday, 12:30, El

Fenix." Setting a specific timeline is the only way to keep from letting your dreams and goals fall under the realm of "someday." They are not going to happen until you set a time to start pursuing them and also plan for a finish date.

Things don't magically happen just because we write them down. I mentioned in a previous chapter that I had asked each of my staff to write down their five-year plan, which we revisited after six months. Some of them were amazed to see how quickly time had slipped away from them without making any progress. I asked them to consider this question: "What am I doing to pursue this dream, to make it happen in my life?" One of Moses' prayers is recorded in the psalms: "Teach us to number our days and recognize how few they are. Help us to spend them as we should" (Ps. 90:12, *TLB*). It is foolish to waste even a single day, especially when a day away from pursuing our dreams could mean we don't realize them at all.

I heard a joke once about a guy who went to the doctor to get the results from an annual exam. His doctor met with him and said, "I'm sorry, Bob, but I've got some bad news for you. The tests show that you have a terminal disease. You only have six months to live." Bob let the news sink in, and then he said, "Is there anything I can do? Are there any experimental drugs or treatment? There has to be something I can try." The doctor thought for a moment. Then he said, "There is one thing. You could move to the country, buy a pig farm and raise pigs. Then you could find a widow who has 14 kids, marry her and bring all of them to live on the pig farm." Bob looked puzzled and asked, "And that will help me live longer?" The doctor said, "No, but it will seem like the longest six months of your life."

That is a light-hearted way of reminding us that our days are numbered. We all have a terminal diagnosis because not a single one of us will live forever. Some have less time than others. Regardless of how much time we do have, we cannot afford to waste another year, month, or even a day. We have to start doing whatever God has for us to do on this earth.

If you had just 30 days left to live—just one month to get your act together—what would you do differently? How would you view time if you knew your last day was just a calendar page away? Every day we wake up and breathe is valuable, and it should count for something.

I've read statistics that the average person spends six hours a day watching TV. Six hours a day for a month adds up to 180 hours, or seven-and-a-half days! Let's go back to the question of how you would spend your time if you knew you only had 30 days left. Now subtract seven-and-a-half days from that for television time. You're left with just under three weeks to live. Doesn't that give you some perspective on what it means when we don't live on purpose and with purpose?

We often wonder why we aren't closer to our dreams, why we aren't farther along toward our goals, why it feels as though we are spinning our wheels and repeating the same thing year after year. The apostle Paul wrote, "We beg you, please don't squander one bit of this marvelous life God has given us" (2 Cor. 6:1, *THE MESSAGE*). Why? Because your time is your life. When we waste time, we waste our life. Pope Paul VI said, "Somebody should tell us right at the start of our lives that we're dying, then we might live life to the limit every minute of every day. . . . Do it, I say, whatever you want to do, do it now. There are only so many tomorrows."

What's Your Plan?

Do you have a plan? If not, it's time to start developing one right now. You'll find that you are the most disciplined in areas where

105

your goals are outlined. Doesn't that make sense? Who would feel like taking on a task when he or she wasn't sure what to do, how to do it or when it was supposed to be finished? Add confusion over why he or she was doing it in the first place and you would have a recipe for procrastination and, ultimately, failure.

Years ago, I went through a period where I felt as though everything in my life was falling apart. My circumstances took a turn for the worse. I didn't have a sense of purpose; I didn't have a plan, any goals or a vision. I spent most days feeling sorry for myself. If it hadn't been for Kassidi, I don't know what would have kept me going, or even kept me getting up in the morning. It was having her that forced me to say to myself every day, *I don't want my daughter to see me crying. I am going to get up with a smile on my face. I am going to act as if everything is fine.* But I knew I couldn't fake it much longer.

After I dropped Kassidi off at school one morning, I returned home and sat on my stairs, sobbing with my head in my hands. I cried out, "God, I don't even know why I'm here. I don't know what I'm supposed to do."

I was desperate for peace. I wanted it more than anything in the world because my mind was so tormented. I was miserable. In fact, I was heartbroken and in pain. I had so much fear in my life I hadn't realized was there. I remember feeling so beaten down and defeated from all of that junk that the thought of looking at a calendar stressed me out. I didn't want to do it. How can you look at something that lays out the future when you don't even know what you are living for today? How can you plan anything for the next week? How can you look at holidays or vacations when you haven't got a clue what you're doing in *this* moment?

Suddenly, the words of Proverbs 29:18 rushed to my awareness: "Where there is no vision the people perish" (*KJV*). It hit me that I was sitting there perishing. Then I remembered the words of a marriage counselor Rodney and I had talked to one time. He told us, "You fight fear with a plan. If you are going somewhere that you have never been before, and you have a fear that you are going to get lost, you don't get into your car without having a plan. You make sure you have a map. You make sure you have a cell phone. And, of course, you take with you the phone number for your destination. This way, if you get lost, you have a plan, a backup plan, and a failsafe. You are totally prepared for what may come. Your plan overrides your fears."

In that moment, I experienced a breakthrough. I needed a plan because I was facing a number of fears. I began to consider how I could apply that wisdom to my particular situation. I sat down at my desk and began to make a list of the most important areas of my life and the things I needed to change.

I wrote down five things. First, I wrote down that I needed a plan for my faith, to solidify my relationship with God. Second, I realized I needed a plan for my family, to structure my home life. Third, I needed a plan for my finances, to secure our future. Fourth, I needed a plan for my fitness, to stabilize my health. And, fifth, I needed a plan for my free time and my friends, to support my personal growth.

I needed to first establish a plan for my faith. I committed to making changes for 21 days. Instead of formulating a vague plan of attack—which I had done at the beginning of every year before this day—I decided to think about it. I meditated on this goal and asked myself, *What does this mean? How do I measure my progress? How do I successfully say, "Yep, I did it. I got closer to God"?* Is it by the number of goose bumps I get in church on Sunday morning? Or by counting how many minutes longer I've prayed today compared to last year?

107

The problem we often encounter in setting goals is that we make such broad declarations that we don't know where to start. And we certainly can't manage to accomplish on intentions only. If we don't break down our goals into realistic steps, it's too daunting to look at them after we write them down. I can say this from personal experience.

That day, I didn't write down my goals so they could take up space on a piece of paper. They mattered because I needed to overcome some big issues in my life. I needed peace and security. I needed to build my faith. The apostle John wrote, "Every child of God can defeat the world, and our faith is what gives us this victory" (1 John 5:4, *CEV*). It takes faith to overcome all of the challenges we will encounter. Faith is nothing more than trusting God. But how do you get faith? The Bible says faith comes by continually hearing the Word of God (see Rom. 4:17).

I made a goal to immerse myself in the Word. I snuck over to my mom and dad's house while they were out of town and went through their library. I took the audio route rather than reading a book, because reading (at least to me) takes a little more effort. You have to stop everything you are doing to focus on reading. But you can multitask while listening to recorded messages. You can fold laundry, do your make-up, cook dinner and play with the kids, all while hearing the Word of God.

I gathered a bunch of messages by Lester Sumrall, Mac Hammond, Joyce Meyer, Jerry Savelle (my dad), and several others, and took them home. If I had looked at this massive stack of sermons without any direction, I would have felt ridiculous and overwhelmed. But I had a plan. I intended to chip away at the list of messages a little at a time. I selected one CD and determined the best time of day for me to listen to it—in the morning while getting ready. No one would be around to distract me or keep me from absorbing the message. I planned to listen to the CDs every day for 21 days. If I could do this consistently for that period of time, I could lay the groundwork to create a positive, faith-building habit for life.

My biggest motivator was that I yearned to see a change in my life. Still, it wasn't easy. In the beginning, I even had to put a note on my bathroom counter, "Push play!" It wasn't a habit for me yet. I had to remind myself to do this until it became second nature. I would go into the bathroom each morning, see my note and remember, *Oh yeah!* Then I would push play, jump in the shower and listen while I went through my morning ritual.

I have to be honest. Initially I didn't notice any change. I was a little disappointed, but I kept on hitting play each morning. Soon, I didn't need the note to prompt me. I got out of bed as soon as the alarm sounded, walked to the bathroom, pushed play and turned on the shower almost as if on autopilot.

Eventually, my goals got bigger. I had the habit down. It was time to expand. I wanted to build my faith more than the previous day. I resolved to spend a little more time hearing God's Word each day. Even if it was an extra five minutes, it was still an improvement. I was growing in my faith and growing closer to God. This is how I started my plan. I strongly believe it was the only way to get my life back on track.

The neat thing about hearing the Word regularly is that it has a positive impact on you even when you aren't aware of it. It is not like listening to music, where you are simply moved by the beat or sentiment or beauty of a song. The Word gets down deep on the inside of you. It starts changing you, even though you don't see it. Every time you hear the Word, your spirit is

109

being charged. It is being fed. It is getting stronger. And the stronger your spirit gets, the weaker your flesh becomes.

I began to look for other opportunities to hear God's Word outside of getting ready for the day. I could listen to messages while driving to work and on my way home. Then I was listening to the Word while I relaxed in the bath at night. Those CDs were with me wherever I went. I was spiritually hungry. The more I learned, the more I wanted to know. I was growing in a measurable way because I could feel myself drawing closer to God. My plan was leading me right to my goal.

Create Realistic Goals

Your goals must be realistic. Don't be extreme in your thinking and say, "I'm going to listen to the Word every morning, and then I'm going to pray for an hour. After that, I'm going to read the whole New Testament, and then I'm going to . . ." (you get the drift). Doing too much too soon isn't practical. It's going to quickly overwhelm you and you'll give up, probably sooner rather than later. Make a plan that is doable and will encourage you to be consistent.

We all know that too much change at one time, even positive change, can be stressful and disruptive. Pace yourself and try to get one habit mastered before tackling another. It only takes 21 days to break a habit, so you will still progress toward your dreams one step at a time. But if you try too much at the same time, you are not likely to advance.

For example, you might decide to take up running because you want to drop a few pounds. Say that on the first day of meeting your fitness goals, you run five miles. It might go okay. You might even feel great and have a better time than you expected. But the next morning, you wake up sore and exhausted, and you decide to give yourself a day off. That one day of rest turns into three or four, and then you think, *I blew it. I messed up the whole thing. I give up.* The problem isn't that you aren't capable of achieving your goal; it's that you set an unrealistic one. You weren't ready to take on so much so soon, and you set yourself up for failure.

You need to approach that goal differently. You need to break it up into manageable steps. When you set a goal, always ask yourself two questions: (1) *How much?* and (2) *By when?* In other words, how much will it take to accomplish my goal, and when will I reach it? Using the same example, you might want to start working on your goals first by getting some advice from your doctor. Then, start walking a couple times a week until you find you can do that without getting tired. Then you can either extend the length of your walk or you can pick up the pace and start jogging. Once you've conquered that level, increase your speed and your distance. All through these steps you are building up strength and stamina. The change in your body will become noticeable and will motivate you to keep climbing upward. You don't have to start out running a marathon. You just have to get to the end of the block, and then the next one, and then the next.

Remember that I said you have to assign a time to go after your dreams? I actually put what I call a "time map" in my dream book. If you've never used this, it will change your life. A time map is a snapshot of your day and helps you pinpoint when you're going to go after your dreams and goals. It is also very effective for helping to break down your goals into bite-sized chunks that keep you on track and moving forward.

Then you must designate a realistic time to accomplish what you've set out to do. When you set a goal, you often forget to determine a time of day to go after your goal or you leave it to chance. It's unrealistic to think you will get to your goals each day if you don't set aside time for them. Life happens, and unexpected demands pop up. If you don't plan for your dreams and incorporate them into your To-Do list, they will get pushed aside for errands, phone calls or mindless distractions.

Just as you need to determine an assigned time to review your dreams, do the same for your goals. Look at your schedule and figure out a realistic time to work on them. If you've settled on mornings to start writing your book, for instance, but your home is chaotic with the kids running around getting ready for school, while you make breakfast and lunches, that's probably not a good time. You wouldn't be able to focus. Instead, choose to write on your lunch hour or after everyone is in bed. If you are an early riser and find your brain doesn't function as well after dinner, get up a little earlier and write while the house is still quiet.

Maybe you will have to rely on someone else to help you accomplish your goals. Maybe your dream requires going back to school, and you have to fit your schedule around your classes. It isn't realistic to create your own routine outside of your school schedule. The point is, if your goals don't fit in with the rest of your day, they won't get done. So make practical plans to make time to pursue your dreams and accomplish your goals.

Hit Obstacles Head-on

A number of things will get in the way and interfere with the plans you make. Some of these things can be avoided with a well-conceived strategy; but other obstacles you can neither anticipate nor entirely remove. So, what do you do then? You pray, and you figure out a way around the obstacles; and then you trust God to lead you through. If He has purposed for you to do something, He will make a way.

As you start setting goals for working toward your dream, you might encounter a financial hurdle, scheduling conflicts or relationship challenges. I have found, however, that one of the biggest obstacles you will face is of a spiritual nature. I am warning you right now that Satan is going to toy with your mind. He is going to manipulate your thoughts and try to defeat you within your mind. He will try to plant thoughts in your head like the following: *I can't drink water because I don't have any. I can't listen to the sermon because my iPod is broken. I can't write this chapter because I don't know what I want to write. I can't pray because I'm never alone.*

There will be a million excuses not to do what you set out to do, but it only takes one good reason to keep going. The only way you can get your flesh under the control of your spirit is by setting your goals, keeping them in front of you, putting the Word of God in your mouth, and speaking that Word out, declaring, "I can do this in Jesus' name."

What happened when Jesus was in the boat with His disciples and said, "Let's get to the other side of the lake"? A storm came. What did Jesus do at that point? Did He say they should turn around, since the weather turned bad? No. Did He panic and worry? No. Did He throw His hands up in surrender and say, "I give up"? No. He defeated the storm. He spoke to it. He confronted the obstacle head-on.

Follow Jesus' example. When challenges arise and you are tempted to find reasons to stop working toward your dream, speak to that area of your life with the Word of God. Face down that obstacle with prayer and faith. Walk through, over or around the towering mountain with confidence that God has put you on this path and you are supposed to finish this

113

course. If you find yourself saying, "I don't have time," look your-self in the eye—go straight to a mirror, if you have to—and say, "Yes, I do have time!" Start brainstorming. Figure out areas in your schedule that you can shift. Look for tasks that can be streamlined or multitasked. Consider where you are wasting time on fruitless activities. Find the time to do what's most important.

Don't let Satan convince you that what you are doing right now is enough to get you where you want to be. I've already men-tioned that the definition of insanity is repeating the same activ-ity but expecting different results. That's what Satan wants you to do. He wants you to run in circles and get nowhere. Reject his manipulation. Turn away from his discouragement. Keep press-ing on toward your dreams.

You will be tempted to get stressed and overwhelmed by how far you have to go and how much work it might take to achieve your goals. When I first started imagining, I used to crumble un-der the pressure. I was at the starting point and already feeling behind. I would go to conferences and hear speakers rattle off facts, stats and inspiring quotes about thinking big and follow-ing your dreams. I'd think, *I'll never catch up to where I should be!* But you know where success begins? With doing one thing. For example, reading one book. One page at a time.

How badly do you want to see change in your life? Do what you need to do. Push yourself. Do something different. Stretch yourself.

Do you need to learn a foreign language?

Do you need to develop more advanced skills in a particular area?

Do you need to get your body into better physical shape?

Do you need to broaden your computer skills?

Do you need to learn a musical instrument?

Do you need to take a writing class?

I like to encourage people to set a goal of doing something productive for at least 20 minutes each day. Most of us can give up that amount of time to do something that will bring lasting change. I've said before that 20 minutes a day comes out to 10 hours a month. That's it! You might be 20 minutes a day away from acquiring a new skill that could revolutionize your finances and move you to a higher income level. Here are some suggestions of what you can achieve in only 20 minutes:

- Study a foreign language during your commute to work each day.
- Give up watching a television show and use that time to organize a room in your house.
- Spend time during your lunch hour to read a motivational book or one chapter of the Bible.
- Get up a little earlier and pray before you head off to work.
- Clean up after dinner and wake up in the morning to a spotless kitchen.
- Write a chapter of your book.
- Clean out your car.
- Go for a walk.

115

Go Out Armed for Battle

It should come as no surprise that you may have a fight on your hands when you commit to fulfilling God's purpose for your life. Prepare yourself for this fight. We have spent some time exploring how to grow your faith. I want to make it clear that spending time in the Word is the best ammunition you can have to win the daily fight. Starting each day in prayer and meditating on Scripture will get you ready for anything you nt encounter. It will likely be an uphill journey to your eams, so move forward equipped with the Word in your neart, prayer on your lips and a mindset that God is leading the way and this is what you are supposed to do.

You may have heard your grandparents, parents or even a teacher say that nothing in life worth having comes easy. That means our dreams are usually achieved by struggle and a determination not to give up. Don't let a few dips in the road keep you from that dream you believe you were put here to do. Don't let Satan rob you of the material, emotional and spiritual riches God intends you to have. Sure, the devil is a powerful enemy, but when you are aligned with God, you are stronger. The first goal you should set for yourself is to remind yourself daily that your dreams are worth the effort. And every goal you set after that is for the purpose of taking you one step closer to them.

Making S.M.A.R.T. Goals

We've covered what S.M.A.R.T. goals are and talked about the role of creating goals in pursuing your dreams. Write down what each of these terms—specific, measurable, attainable, realistic, timely—means to you. If you've thought of a dream you want to get started on now, fill in each blank with a specific goal for that dream.

Specific—What are the details of your dream? What do you want? How do you want it? When do you want it?

Measurable—How can you measure progress toward your dream? In what ways can you quantify your achievements?

_____

_____

_____

_____

Attainable—How can you make your dream attainable? What can you do to equip yourself for the journey to achieving your dream?

_____

_____

_____

117

Realistic—What realistic goals can you set for working toward your dream? How do they fit with your plan and your schedule?

_____

_____

_____

_____

Timely—What is the timeframe for your dream? What are the benchmarks for progress and the deadline for completion?

_____

_____

_____

_____

Chapter 5

INITIATE ACTION NOW

Things may come to those who wait, but only the things
left by those who hustle.
ABRAHAM LINCOLN

Just sitting around, wishing things would change, accomplishes little. Taking action is the only way to have the things we dream of having. Even making a detailed plan the way I showed you in chapter 4 means nothing if you don't implement it. All of the steps you have learned so far look great on paper, but they won't take you anywhere if you don't do anything with them. Now that you have found the excitement to dream and are allowing that inspiration to flow in you, the next step is to take that incredible, life-changing feeling and use it to propel you into action.

Let's look at a story from the Bible found in Luke 5. Jesus was ministering in Capernaum, and a large crowd was listening to Him. A paralyzed man who needed healing wanted to get to Jesus, but he couldn't get through the throngs of people: "When they could not find a way to do this because of the crowd, they went up on the roof and lowered him on his mat through the tiles into the middle of the crowd, right in front of Jesus. When Jesus saw their faith, he said, 'Friend, your sins are forgiven' " (Luke 5:19-20).

These men were determined! They had a specific goal in mind and did not let the obstacle of a crowd and lack of a clear path stand in their way. Notice how the Scripture says, "When Jesus *saw* their faith." How can you see faith when it's an internal thing? Is it even possible to evidence? Jesus saw their faith through their *action*. He recognized their faith through their belief that He could heal their friend and their action to make it happen.

The content of this chapter is a call to action. I want to motivate you to move forward toward your dreams in the knowledge that God can do extraordinary things when you believe enough to step out in faith.

Not all roadblocks are bad. Sometimes they are put in our path to protect us. But we all have a tendency to let roadblocks deter us from our path. If we see them and stop moving forward, and then lose our momentum altogether, they prevent us from reaching our destination. Don't let obstacles end your journey. Find a way around them so you can get back on track.

The men in the Luke 5 story didn't let the massive number of people listening to Jesus teach discourage them. They didn't throw up their hands and say, "Oh well, we tried," and give up. They had something pressing to do, so they refused to quit. They didn't go home without completing their mission. They were pro*active*.

The second *I* in *IMAGINE BIG* stands for "initiate action now." I want you to discover the wisdom found in the Bible to wisely utilize your time. As I encouraged in the last chapter, don't take for granted a single moment of your life. Choose to make every day count. Find your purpose and go after it.

When God expands your imagination and gives you a bigger vision for your life, there is no room for procrastination. If you spend even a minute putting off your goals—vowing to "do it tomorrow"—you are wasting a minute that becomes an hour, which turns into a month and often stretches into a year of the valuable and limited time God has given you; this is time that you are supposed to be using to work toward fulfilling your purpose.

I've experienced firsthand the frustration and emptiness of living a life of procrastination. I've also experienced the freedom and joy that come from living a proactive, purpose-filled life. I want you to experience that same freedom and joy in your life. One way I'll help you get there is by giving you a 30-day "Do It Now" challenge found at the end of this chapter. This plan will quicken your steps toward living your dreams and build your confidence as you begin pursuing your goals.

121

Faith Without Works

Having a dream is an inspiring and wonderful thing. It fills you with hope and encouragement. It gives you direction. It helps you understand why you are here. It elevates your faith to endure even the rockiest of roads on your journey. Yet, if you don't put action behind these truths, they mean nothing.

The apostle James wrote, "Faith apart from works is useless" (Jas. 2:20, *ESV*). *THE MESSAGE* version reads as follows: "Do I hear you professing to believe in the one and only God, but then observe you complacently sitting back as if you had done something wonderful? That's just great. Demons do that, but what good does it do them? Use your heads! Do you suppose for a minute that you can cut faith and works in two and not end up with a corpse on your hands?"

I love the way this Scripture points out that any of us can say we believe, but the work we do proves how much faith we actually have. Here's one more version of James 2:20, from *The*

Amplified Bible: "Are you willing to be shown [proof], you foolish (unproductive, spiritually deficient) fellow, that faith apart from [good] works is inactive and ineffective and worthless?" Faith without works is dead. Don't sit back and do nothing, expecting your dreams to just happen. Fulfilling your purpose requires, and even demands, your effort.

I've already covered planning, which is incredibly important. Starting out without a course of action is, at the very least, going to delay your progress; at its worst it can derail your journey altogether. And sometimes you can get bogged down with planning, analyzing and thinking, and never take any action. That said, a plan is useless if it is never put into action. Thomas Edison said, "Opportunity is missed by most people because it comes dressed in overalls and looks like work." Don't let any opportunity slip by because you fail to put your faith into action.

If you keep telling yourself, "That's a great idea; I will do it tomorrow," you will usually find yourself pushing it out even further. Statements like "I'll do that on Monday" or "I'll do that after the first of the year" eventually become "I'll do that *someday*." Do it today!

Do something to bring your dreams into reality even if it's one small task on your goal list. Start moving forward. If your dream is to go back to school, go online and research programs. Request a course catalog. Inquire about financial aid. Fill out the application. Get something done.

If your aspiration is to lose weight, don't put it off any longer. Start with the meal you are about to eat. Think about what's on your plate and consider whether or not it will help you reach your goals.

We are all a work in progress. Don't get discouraged because you have a setback. The key to success is forward movement. As long as you are moving forward, you are making progress. Don't scrap the whole thing because you had one misstep. That's just another form of procrastination. There's no need to delay action because of a bad day, a mistake or a slip-up. Get back up and try again.

Great Gifts Come with Great Responsibility

This journey is going to take work. You don't get to sit back and say, "Okay, God, make it happen!" This is a team effort between you and God. He's not going to do everything for you. You are expected to participate. "Great gifts mean great responsibilities; greater gifts, greater responsibilities!" (Luke 12:48, *THE MESSAGE*). The faith you have in God to do great things for you and through you comes with great responsibility, which means effort on your part.

123

To have faith means that you have a vision of the end result before that result can be seen in the natural realm. I've said that everything starts in your mind. When you start dreaming, all you may have at first is an image. The apostle Paul wrote, "For we walk by faith and not by sight" (2 Cor. 5:7, *KJV*). That means we must be confident in what we see in our spirit and we shouldn't be swayed by what we see with our physical eyes. That takes some pretty strong faith, doesn't it?

When everything around you looks like it will never come to pass, you need faith like never before. Satan is not going to stop hounding you. He will tell you over and over, "Your dreams are ridiculous. They're stupid. You're foolish for even indulging these dreams. Who do you think you are?" You can take heart knowing that when that much effort is being made to discourage you from pursuing your dreams, you're probably on the right track.

Stay encouraged and keep believing that God can use you. That the dream you have is not pointless. That it's not crazy. That God has plans for you—good plans designed specifically for you. And if the people around you don't understand your dreams or support you, it's okay. These plans—these dreams—were intended for you, not for someone else.

You have to develop your faith to such a degree that you can confess Hebrews 11:1 with confidence: "Now faith is confidence in what we hope for and assurance about what we do not see." Faith is the key to having the confidence to believe for the dreams you don't see manifesting yet. Maybe when you look at the zero balance in your bank account you are convinced that is all you can ever expect. Or you look at your worn-out car, or your drunken husband, or your overweight body, or the job you hate and you believe you have to settle for life as it is now. That's not faith. But when you begin to meditate on God's Word, listen to inspiring, faith-filled messages and let God birth dreams in you, you will begin to see yourself with confidence, boldness and courage. You will visualize yourself stepping out and doing the things that seem impossible. You can imagine your life changing.

Your whole perspective changes for the better. You see an image on the inside of you and you begin to imagine a better life. You begin to imagine a bank account with a cushion of $5,000. You begin to imagine a new car. You begin to imagine a husband free from alcohol and serving God. You begin to imagine a fit and trim body. You begin to imagine a fulfilling job where you can engage your deepest passions and God-given gifts.

That's the beginning of your dream journey. Now you have to add action to your faith. Make a dream book. Set some goals. Start taking steps toward your dreams. Initiate action now. A helpful way of looking at this part of your plan is that you are changing from being reactive to your circumstances to being proactive. If you are being proactive, you will take steps toward your dream in anticipation of it becoming your reality. But when you are reactive, you only respond to things that are happening to you; those movements are less deliberate and usually delay progress toward your dream.

In Matthew 14, where we read that the disciples were in a boat when a horrible storm came up, Peter saw a man, or what he thought might be an apparition that looked like Jesus, out on the water. Peter asked the "apparition" if He was really Jesus to call him out of the boat and onto the water. When Jesus said, "Come," Peter began walking on the water. He was acting by faith. Not long after, however, Peter got distracted by the natural—by the stormy waves all around him. What he saw with his physical eyes frightened him, and the fear grew bigger in his heart. When he took his eyes off of Jesus, Peter began focusing on what was happening around him, and that's when he started to sink.

When your dreams and goals look like they will never happen, you have to kick it up a notch and take action. You have to stir up your faith. I'm telling you again, Satan is never going to let up. He is never going to let you pursue your dreams without a fight. You have to learn to keep your faith activated. Put one foot in front of the other and initiate action.

Your Dream Works

In the classic success book *Think and Grow Rich*, the legendary story is told of award-winning motion picture director Steven Spielberg, who dreamed of being a movie director from childhood. He began making amateur films with a little camera

125

when he was just a boy. That dream never left him, and he built his life around making it happen. Spielberg's first full-length film was *The Sugarland Express*. Even though it didn't do very well at the box office, it received critical acclaim and won a "Best Screenplay" award at the 1974 Cannes Film Festival.

Spielberg's big break came a year later when he discovered the book *Jaws*. A particular movie studio had already decided to produce the film adaptation and had chosen a well-known director to film it. Spielberg desperately wanted to make this movie. Despite the financial failure of *The Sugarland Express*, his self-confidence had not diminished, and he persuaded the producers to allow him to take on the project. It was not an easy assignment. There were multiple technical and budget problems during the filming process. However, when *Jaws* was released, it broke box-office records. Within a month of its release, the film had raked in $60 million at the box office, *and* the critics loved it.

Over the next few years, Spielberg directed several movies, including hits like the *Indiana Jones* series, *The Color Purple*, *Empire of the Sun*, and *E.T.*, as well as *Jurassic Park*, which would become one of the most successful movies in film history. Later, he and two other Hollywood moguls created their own production company called Dreamworks (what an appropriate name!). Spielberg didn't wait for something to happen. He initiated action. He refused to let anything stand in his way. He fought against the odds. He did not let disappointments deter him from his mission.[1]

Do something, lest you do nothing. I've heard life coach, writer and speaker Peter Daniels say, "So many people say, 'I'm just waiting on God. I'm just waiting on God.' But God is not behind you. He's ahead of you. He's waiting on you." God is out in front, making the way for you. All you have to do is start moving toward Him. When you start taking action steps, your dreams become more visible. It's the way it works. Things start happening. Momentum builds. Opportunities reveal themselves and relationships are formed to help bring about your dreams.

As you initiate action, new ideas will come to life. It's like a baby taking her first step. The first is usually the hardest. As she sets out on this milestone, she will fall, but she will always get back up and do it again. Eventually, babies learn balance and begin covering more ground. Then the walk turns into a run. Once that happens, there's no stopping them.

The same phenomenon happens when you start taking steps toward your dreams. You may stumble. You may even fall down. But remember, failure isn't in the fall; it's in not getting back up and trying again. So get into motion. Book that cruise you've always wanted to go on. Update your résumé. Write that book. Meet with a realtor. Save money, even if it's a few dollars a week. Join the gym. Record the CD. Volunteer at the shelter. Preach the message. Nothing is going to happen until you take action.

Think back to the story in Luke 5 about the four men helping their paralyzed friend get Jesus' attention in a crowd of people. Let's consider their actions again. When they found their way to the place where Jesus was preaching, there were so many people they could barely move, let alone see Him. Instead of saying, "It must not be God's will for us to get to Jesus. He must have closed the door," they found a creative solution and kicked open the door. It says these four men "sought means" to bring their friend to Jesus (Luke 5:18). The word "means" is *plural*, not singular. They tried more than one approach. The *New International Version* translation says, "When they could not find a way to do this because of the crowd, they went up on the roof" (v. 19). I like the symbolism in that version. They went up higher. They went the extra mile. They proved the old saying that success is 10 percent inspiration and 90 percent perspiration. Figure out what you need to do, and do it. And don't stop even if a door closes on your way. Push it open.

It's Not Easier Tomorrow

Sometimes we get the mistaken notion that it's easier to put something off until the next day. We can find ourselves sliding down the slippery slope of a "tomorrow" mentality. In most cases, postponing a task makes it more difficult. You put more pressure on yourself because your deadline is now tighter. Also, you may now have people breathing down your neck because your procrastination affects them to a degree. Maybe they made plans around your commitment. Maybe someone is counting on you for that report or waiting for you to finish that paperwork. You can also miss an opportunity because you wait too long. The bottom line is, when you put things off, you risk paying a costly price.

Is procrastination a weak area in your life? Then start with small actions. Tackle just one task you keep putting off. Everyone is prone to delaying the unpleasant things on their To-Do lists, such as scrubbing the grout in the bathroom or weeding the garden, but these are good illustrations of things that only get worse when you put off doing them. I want you to conquer procrastination. Make time to do the things you keep putting off. Get them out of the way. Trust me, when you complete these little tasks, a huge weight will release from your shoulders. You will feel free. Imagine what even greater relief you will experience when you stop procrastinating on the big things, like what God is telling you to do with your life!

Let's look at a couple of procrastinators in the Bible—one example from the Old Testament and one from the New Testament. A classic example in the Old Testament is Pharaoh, the Egyptian leader who enslaved the nation of Israel and refused to grant their freedom. God commanded Moses to tell Pharaoh to let His people go. Each time Moses approached the king, Pharaoh refused. He was merely postponing the inevitable. Finally, God sent plagues to cover the entire land of Egypt. He turned water to blood. He sent massive infestations of fleas, lice and frogs. You'd think that would be more than enough to make Pharaoh surrender, but no. So God sent more plagues. He inflicted diseases on the livestock and covered the Egyptian people with boils. Then He poured down hail from heaven and covered the land with darkness.

Finally, Pharaoh requested a meeting with Moses and his right-hand man, Aaron. The king asked them to plead with God on his behalf. Moses told Pharaoh over and over what it would take to stop the suffering he and the Egyptian people were enduring. After each plague, Pharaoh had the choice to let the people of Israel go and be delivered from the plagues that were wreaking havoc on his people and land. He could have said to Moses, "Okay, the Israelites can go free. Not tomorrow. Not next week. Now." Yet, the Egyptian king procrastinated. He chose to spend another night in bondage and, as a result, suffered the consequences. (Read the whole story in Genesis 7–12.)

You may think Pharaoh was foolish, and though that's true, don't many of us do the same thing? How many of us put off our deliverance from alcohol, smoking, drugs, excessive eating or unhealthy relationships? How many of us refuse to say, "I'm fed up with this mess, and I'm getting help now!" How many of us keep living in bondage to a plague of our own choosing?

· · · · ·

129

· · · · ·

Do you want to repeat this year what you did last year? Or do you want to instead be able to say, "Thank You, Lord, for what You've done in my life. I am not the person I used to be. My life is different than it was before." Our goal should be that when we one day stand before God, we can say, "Lord, I did exactly what You assigned me to do during my lifetime." If you stop procrastinating and initiate action now, you *can* say that. You *can* complete His assignment. Decide today what it is that you need to do, and do it.

Why We *Procrastinate*

Organizational and productivity expert Julie Morgenstern explains in her book *Time Management from the Inside Out* some of the psychological reasons we might put some things off. Let's look at those in detail.

1. *You have unclear goals and priorities.* Without clearly defined goals, it is nearly impossible to follow through on your plans or to make decisions on how or where to spend your time. Any little distraction that comes along takes you away from what you need to do. Without a specific goal and a detailed plan of attack, you will never escape the long list of excuses to get started.

2. *You are a "Conquistador of Chaos."* Do you thrive on being busy, on getting things done, on checking off one accomplishment after the next? A Conquistador (conqueror) of Chaos might not sound

like a bad thing, and completing your To-Do list should be a positive attribute. But, being too busy can also interfere with the pursuit of your dreams. You might be a great crisis manager, but that doesn't mean you should look for disasters. If you are letting everyone else's drama distract you from what you are supposed to do, you are procrastinating in your own life. You are avoiding completing the goals that will get you to your dreams.

3. *You have a fear of failure.* If you know what your goals are, but you're not actually working on them, you might have a fear of failure. Going after your dreams only to find out you're incapable of achieving them can be a debilitating fear. Many times it is easier to avoid making the effort so you can blame it on life circumstances rather than risk failure. There is also a lot of intimidation wrapped up in maintaining success if you achieve it. You are always facing another potential failure, and that pressure can be overwhelming. This expectation of disappointment forces you to stop trying before you ever get started, and your dreams go unrealized.

4. *You have a fear of down time.* If the idea of taking a day off, taking some time for yourself, and slowing down enough to relax sends you into a panic, you need down time. It can be difficult to actually take time off because you feel you're not being productive. Maybe you are the type of person who feels that an empty calendar is a sign of failure. It could be that you are keeping your schedule packed and your mind cluttered to avoid thinking

131

about larger things like your true calling and what you should be doing to fulfill that. Avoiding this bigger job by doing a lot of little ones is holding you back from your dream.

5. *You have a fear of completion.* Some people have a hard time making progress with their goals and keep starting projects, bouncing back and forth between all of them, never finishing one. This can be motivated by the concern that when the project ends so does their usefulness. The sad thing is you never get to truly enjoy the feeling of accomplishment. That results in a loss of energy and self-esteem, because you always feel bad about yourself for never finishing a project. Putting off completing a project keeps you from your dreams because you don't have the momentum to get there.

6. *You have a need for perfection.* Perfectionists feel compelled to do everything at the same level of excellence, which usually comes from a need for approval. Maybe you fear criticism, humiliation, or harsh judgment. Or it could be that you feel more secure when everything seems to be under your control. Whatever drives your need for perfection, it is a major obstacle to realizing your dreams. If you continue to wait until you have the ideal circumstances or pristine conditions, you will never get started because nothing in life is perfect.[2]

A second illustration of procrastination from the Bible is found in John 5. The scene takes place at the pool of Bethesda.

According to tradition, when the water would move, the first person into the pool would get healed. Consequently, the pool was regularly crowded with disabled people—the lame, blind, deaf, paralytic—hoping for a chance to be healed. One man, an invalid, had been waiting there for 38 years. One day, Jesus was visiting the pool and, knowing this man's situation, stopped to talk to him. He asked a question, "Do you want to get well?" It warranted an obvious response, but surprisingly, the man didn't say yes. He started rambling on with excuses: *I have no one to help me. Whenever I try to get in, someone gets there before me.* Jesus then told him to pick up his mat and walk. The man did and was healed in an instant.

I find it interesting that Jesus had to ask him if he wanted to get well. But if you think about it, the question was a good one. After all, the man had been sitting by the pool for 38 years, waiting for someone to come along, waiting for someone to pick him up, waiting for somebody to solve his problem. In that amount of time he should have been able to do something to help himself and change his predicament. He could have asked everyone who came by for help until someone was finally willing to step in. Instead, he sat there, suffering in silence.

The message for us today is (1) you have to get up; (2) you have to pick up the mess you've been lying around in all this time; (3) you have to start walking, moving, putting one foot in front of the other. You have to *do* something.

What is Jesus saying to you about your dreams? Is He telling you to write that music and start singing? Is He calling you to pick up that Bible and start preaching? Maybe He is urging you to dust off your computer skills and get that job. Or get up off your bottom and get to the gym. Or start doing the research to build that company. Whatever it is that God

· · · · ·

133

· · · · ·

wants you to do, don't sit by and wait for someone else to come along and motivate you. Don't wait for a friend or a family member to outline your life plan. It's not going to happen. No one else can map out God's blueprint for your life, and they shouldn't do that anyway. Why would you want someone else to receive that personal calling from God for you? This is your dream, your purpose, your life.

You might be saying, "Terri, 38 years is a long time. I haven't put anything off that long." Maybe you haven't procrastinated for almost four decades; nonetheless, I want to challenge you to think about your life and the things that may hold you in bondage. I'll admit I'm still dealing with issues that have plagued me for years. I'm not naive. If I don't get up and start working on a solution, I could be looking at 10 years of shouldering these burdens. (Which is why I'm initiating action in my own life.)

Consider this: *You* are the only one who will stand before God to give an account for your life—not your mother or father, not your boss or your best friend. Just you. And you're not going to answer for anyone else's life. If God says, "I called you to sing. Why didn't you sing?" will your response be "But I was waiting for somebody to come help me and give me voice lessons"? That won't cut it. God will ask why you didn't sign up for voice lessons, or why you didn't practice or seek opportunities to use the gift He gave you. Fulfilling your purpose doesn't happen just because God gave you a particular ability. And it certainly doesn't manifest just because you write in your dream book, "I'm going to be a Christian singer and I'm going to lead people to Jesus through my songs." It's not enough. You have to initiate action.

Think about the story of Jonah in the Bible. God told him to go to Nineveh and preach to the people there. And what did Jonah do? He went as far in the opposite direction as possible to a place called Tarshish. Most of us know what happened next. Jonah was engulfed by a mess of problems, thrown into a pit of depression and surrounded by storms, feeling completely lost. Then a big fish swallowed him. Finally, he cried out to God, the big fish spat him out and God repeated His command to go to Nineveh. God's plan for Jonah didn't change. His instruction wasn't different. All that happened was that Jonah wasted time. Because he disobeyed God, Jonah spent that time in unnecessary suffering when he could have been enjoying God's blessings.

You can choose to ignore God's direction and even disobey Him, but He is going to keep bringing you back to Him and to what He wants you to do. You can keep trying to delay the inevitable, but God is still going to tell you to go to your Nineveh, because that is what He needs you to do. He wants to help you build a blessing and make your dreams come true.

135

Today Is the Day

God is the great I AM (see Exod. 3:14; John 8:58). He is not the great I Was. God is present tense. Procrastination doesn't fit with the "right now" workings of God. It is a trap of the devil to drag you backward and pull you away from the ultimate plan God has for your life. That's why *now* is the time to make that solid decision to take control of your clock and your calendar, especially when the Spirit moves.

Successful people don't wait when they are inspired to do something. They make a move immediately. I've heard that if you don't act within 24 hours of the inspiration to do something, chances are you never will. You have to act on whatever God is stirring in you. Tell yourself out loud, "Today's the day!"

I recently read about the actor Sylvester Stallone. The most powerful part of his story begins on March 24, 1975, when Chuck Wepner, a relatively unknown 30-to-1 underdog prize-fighter did what no one thought he could do. He went 15 rounds with heavyweight champion Muhammad Ali. In the ninth round, Wepner knocked the champ to the ground, shocking Ali and everyone watching the fight. Though Ali went on to win the fight and retain his title, Wepner came within seconds of defeating his formidable opponent. While this is an extraordinary story, the real inspiration for us is in what happened a thousand miles away.

A struggling actor named Sylvester Stallone saw this fight on TV. Although he had been contemplating the idea of writing a screenplay about a down-and-out fighter getting a title, he thought it was too unrealistic for a movie studio to buy the story. But after seeing Wepner almost pull off what Stallone was imagining, the actor knew he had to write. He started writing that night. Three days later, Stallone had completed the script for the hit movie *Rocky*. The story he almost didn't pursue won three Oscars, including one for Best Picture. It also launched Stallone's multimillion-dollar movie career.[3]

Had Stallone decided to wait until the next day to start writing, he might have lost some of his inspiration, because the fight wasn't fresh in his mind. Maybe the script wouldn't have been as powerful. But he didn't wait. He didn't say, "I'll get serious about this tomorrow." Stallone was determined to "do it now." His entire destiny changed because he acted on an idea. When God places something on your heart and plants it in your mind, you have to act immediately. Don't set aside dreams, visions or goals for a more convenient time or for when you have more confidence. God gave you that inspiration at that time for a reason. Act now.

I have a list of confessions that I recite every morning. One is, "My spirit attracts God-inspired ideas that bring millions of souls and millions of dollars into the kingdom of God." God is giving us ideas all the time, and when we receive them, we have to do something about them in that moment. We can't keep saying "tomorrow." Think about what God is telling you to do. In what areas of your life do you need to get serious? Where do you need to make changes? When you start obeying God and stop procrastinating, you will discover all the wonderful things He has been planning for you.

In 2002, when I was going through the worst time in my life, I heard a minister say in a sermon I was listening to, "Somebody in need is waiting on the other side of your obedience." He said it twice. Each time, that statement hit me right between the eyes. I felt God was telling me, "Wake up, Terri! Get with it. Start making the right decisions and start doing the right thing, because somebody in need is waiting for you to get your act together. Someone is waiting for you to become who I need you to be so I can use you to meet this need." Today, when I meet someone I have ministered to through my books or speaking, and they share their testimony with me, I can't help but think about that day. I think of how this person might have been waiting on the other side of my obedience.

Don't waste another day. Someone may need you, and he or she may not be able to wait a year, a month or even a day for you to get your act together. It's been said that the way you do anything is the way you do everything. If you procrastinate in small areas, it will be a problem in more pressing areas as well. Do you pay your bills late and then have to pay an extra fee? Are you usually late to an appointment or meeting and have to

137

apologize to everyone? Do you return things after the grace period and end up wasting money? Do you file your taxes late and have to pay penalties?

Don't let these bad habits stand in the way of the vision God has given you. Get yourself moving. Put your plan in place. Initiate action now.

"Do It Now" Challenge

When we start a habit of procrastinating in the *little things*, the *big things* of life are usually the next to suffer. If we tend to put things off to the last minute, *we could be putting off the plan God has for our lives as well!*

Here are four principles for initiating action now and getting procrastination out of your life for good:

1. *Make a list of the top 10 things you've delayed getting done.* It could be anything: getting a health checkup, getting the oil changed in your car, calling a friend, or replacing a broken doorknob. Maybe it's filing away your bills or cleaning out a junky closet or finishing a book manuscript.

2. *Put these items on your calendar.* Designate specific times over the next 30 days to work on each task on your list. You don't have to do them all in one day. Incorporate them into your schedule and follow through.

3. *Go through your list one by one.* Take each task, one at a time, and work on it until it's complete. Check tasks off the list so you get the sense of accomplishment that comes from achieving a goal.

4. *Share your progress and feelings with me at www.terri .com/about/contact-us.* You will notice an increase in your confidence as you begin pursuing your goals. When this 30-day challenge is over—and even during it—you will feel exhilarated. As you conquer procrastination in the areas that don't seem significant, it will actually prepare you to take the next step and go after your bigger dreams.

I know firsthand the frustration and emptiness of living a life of procrastination. I also know the freedom and joy that come from living a proactive, purpose-filled life. I want you to experience that same freedom and joy in your life. It's not always easy, but I'm praying you have the inner strength to take the steps to take the "Do It Now" challenge and conquer procrastination today!

139

A wise person does at once, what a fool does at last.
Both do the same thing; only at different times.
LORD ACTON

Chapter 6

No more negativity

Success comes to those who are success-conscious. Failure comes to
those who allow themselves to become failure-conscious.
NAPOLEON HILL

Winners don't waste time in unproductive thought. People fail to achieve because of how they think, not because of their education, who they know, where they were born or how old they are. If you want to change your life, you have to change your negative thinking into positive thoughts. You will never make permanent change until you change your thinking.

People such as Arnold Schwarzenegger, Steven Spielberg, Thomas Edison, Henry Ford, Abraham Lincoln, Ray Kroc and Jim Carrey saw themselves being successful before they ever stepped out and shot for the stars. They enlarged their thinking. They renewed their minds for success. Napoleon Hill said, "Whatever the mind of man can conceive and believe, it can achieve." James Allen said, "A man is literally what he thinks." God's Word says, "As [a man] thinks in his heart, so is he" (Prov. 23:7).

To change your life, you have to change your thinking. Your mind is the most important factor in determining the actions you take. If you change your thinking, your entire life can change!

Norman Vincent Peale once shared a story of some American sailors who were visiting a port in China. As they walked around the harbor, they saw a tattoo parlor with a window display of a variety of ink-inscripted images. One tattoo read "Born to lose." The sailors stepped inside to ask the artist if people really got that tattoo. In a thick Chinese accent, the man replied, "Before tattooed on body, tattooed on mind." You are what you think you are. You will have what you think you will have. You will do what you think you will do.

The *N* in *IMAGINE BIG* stands for "no more negativity." If you're going to develop your faith for big dreams, you have to say what you believe, not what you feel. There's a big difference! We will learn how to identify negative thoughts as they pop up, before they can turn into spoken words and become strongholds. We will find ways to make our thoughts and our speech support our dreams and the action we take to achieve them.

Your mind is like a magnet. You attract what you think. If you think no one likes you, you won't attract friends. If you think you'll never have enough money, you'll always come up short. If you think you're worthless, you're going to attract people who treat you poorly. But if you think the favor of God is on your life, you're going to attract God's favor opening doors for you that no man can shut.

Your life today is the sum total of the thoughts you had yesterday. Bill Chandler says, "Just as a foundation determines the size of the house, your thinking determines the size of your prosperity! If you want to increase the size of your house, you will need to increase the size of your foundation." Is your foundation big enough for what you want to build? Does your thinking support your big dreams? Or are you trying to build a mansion while investing very little into the foundation?

Third John 1:2 says that God desires above all things that we prosper and be in health even as our soul prospers. Your soul is made up of your mind, your will and your emotions. It comprises how you think, what you want and how you feel. It's where your thinking takes place. You could translate the verse this way: "You will prosper and be in health only as (or in direct proportion to the level that) your thinking prospers."

An amazing aspect of our minds is that *we* get to control the ideas that form there. We are in charge of where they go. With a little understanding of how to manage and redirect them when necessary, we have the power to make our thoughts what we need them to be to achieve our dreams.

The Power of Words

An easy way to assess how a person thinks is by listening to what they say. Sometimes people make the mistake of articulating doubts when they start to dream. While they get excited at first, disbelief creeps in at some point and they begin voicing disbelief and negative thoughts: *I can't handle going back to school. I don't have the experience to start a business. There is no way Company X will hire me. I'll never be able to afford that house.*

The apostle Paul wrote, "I believed; therefore I have spoken" (2 Cor. 4:13). It's not enough to think about your imaginings and dreams; you have to speak them. When you begin dreaming of and believing for new things in your life, you will automatically verbalize them. You'll be so excited you can't help but talk about them. Throughout this chapter, I want you to see how powerful your speech is. As we explore the impact the spoken word has on us, we will find the encouragement to stop speaking against our dreams, no matter how impossible they may look.

143

The more time you spend in God's Word, and the more time you read challenging, faith-building books and listen to inspiring sermons, the more you will expand your imagination. You will birth new ideas. You will build confidence. You will believe what Jesus said in Mark 9:23—that everything is possible for one who believes.

Faith is released through words. Throughout the Bible we see that when God wanted something to happen, He spoke it. You have to do the same thing. Your words have everything to do with what your life looks like now and what it can and will look like going forward. You can prophesy your future. Be constant and consistent in speaking what you believe, and never speak against your dream. Neutralize negative speech.

To do that, you have to get your mouth lined up with your imagination. Bestselling self-help author Dr. Daniel Amen said, "Don't believe everything you hear—even in your own mind."[1] Your mind is going to throw everything but the kitchen sink at you as you start opening it up to dream. While a benefit to imagining is seeing more possibilities than you would otherwise not have seen, it also opens up your mind to negative ideas. Along with the big, wonderful dreams that come, worries and small thinking show up. It is important to learn how to filter the messages that come so you know which are useful, which are of God and which are a distraction from the enemy. Unite your mind with the beliefs in your spirit and speak those things.

Jesus said, "For the mouth speaks what the heart is full of. A good man brings good things out of the good stored up in him, and an evil man brings evil things out of the evil stored up in him" (Matt. 12:34-35). Whatever fills our minds eventually consumes our hearts, and it spills over in such a way that we begin speaking it. Whether we are overwhelmed with fear or exploding with excitement, our thoughts and feelings reveal themselves in the way we talk.

We are prone to falling for the messages we hear repeatedly. This can work for us or against us. That's why it's necessary not only to stop speaking negatively against your dreams, but also to give yourself positive messages on a regular basis and fill your mind with affirmation that the dream you have will become a reality.

I've previously referenced Romans 4:17, where the apostle Paul tells us that we serve a God who gives life to the dead and speaks of nonexistent things as if they exist. That's what you're doing when you speak your dreams. You are giving voice to the things that haven't happened yet as if they already have. God spoke this whole world into being by calling things that were not as though they were. Do the same thing. This is how you take charge of your destiny. This is how you start the process of seeing dramatic changes in your life.

145

Shut Out Negative Voices

To grow your belief in your dreams, you need to continue speaking messages of faith to yourself. Satan will try to talk you out of them. He wants more than anything for you to allow what seems impossible to become bigger than what God says is possible. He wants you to feel ridiculous and stupid about believing in your dreams. He wants to convince you that it is a waste of time for you to even put these crazy visions on paper.

I have dreams right now that are so farfetched, audacious and big that I don't have a clue how God is going to make them happen. Satan tells me constantly that I am foolish for continuing to dream and believe. He whispers in my ear, "Who do you think you are that this could happen for you?

What makes you special? Do you know that many other peo-ple had that same dream and failed? What makes you any dif-ferent?" I've learned to keep shutting him up. I've learned to fight him with the Word. I've learned to cut him down with the Sword of the Spirit.

The devil is not the only enemy you have. There's another one closer than you think. One of your worst enemies is your very own mouth. You also have to learn to shut yourself up. You have to eliminate the whispers of doubts, anxieties and fears that come your way. You have to ignore your insecurities, your questions and your arguments to quit.

When we are filled with passion and excitement for God's Word and for the vision He has given us, we begin speaking forth the thoughts, hopes and expectations that come to mind. As you keep focused on your dreams, you will begin speaking those positive confessions out loud. But if you do not keep your dreams in front of you and fill yourself with God's Word, you make room for the enemies—the devil, your own insecurities and others' voices—to fill the void with de-structive words. Your confidence will be shaky and unsettled if you keep speaking doubt, negativity, unbelief and impossi-bilities about your dream.

Don't let what comes out of your mouth take you off track. Keep uttering words of encouragement to yourself, accepting your dream as a done deal. Instead of verbalizing words of fear and hopelessness, speak statements of joy and thankfulness for what God has already done (even if you can't see it yet).

You Get What You Say

Think about how many times a day you tell yourself negative messages like *I can't imagine . . .* or *I don't think I will ever . . .*

or *That could never happen for me*. A few friends and I were out on a beautiful lake. We were admiring a stunning mansion by the shore. It was grand and opulent. I waited to hear if anyone would say, "I can't imagine living in a house like that," because that's what most people think when they see something that seems unattainable. This is the kind of negative talk that prevents us from striving toward, much less realizing our dreams. I want you to get those thoughts out of your mind, once and for all.

Stop speaking destructive words. If you think your dreams are impossible, and you say that out loud, they will be impossible. If you talk about how you'll never have money, you never will have money. If you continually tell yourself that losing weight is so hard, it will be hard. Our words have real power. What we say will be.

Consider how greatly we can be affected by others' words. Their words can wound our spirits deeply, or they can inspire us to do incredible things. They can fill us with deep compassion, or fill us with intense fear. Now think about how heavily influenced you are by that voice in your head. You can talk yourself into or out of just about any mood or decision. You can convince yourself that you are sick when you aren't; and with positive affirmation, you can get better when you're sick.

Speak Life-giving Words

I want to focus now on the positive aspect of how powerful our thoughts are. Humans have the incredible ability to overcome inconceivable odds through the life-giving and changing messages we tell ourselves.

Let's revisit Mark 11:23-24, which says, "I tell you the truth, if anyone says to this mountain, 'Go throw yourself into the sea' and does not doubt in his heart, but believes that what he says will happen, it will be done for him." Read what *THE MESSAGE* says in that passage of Scripture: "Jesus was matter of fact, 'Embrace this God life, really embrace it, and nothing will be too much for you. This mountain, for instance, just say 'Go jump in the lake' no shuffling or shilly-shallying, and it's as good as done." This biblical text taps into how powerful we are when we are aligned with God, when we "embrace this God life." When we are connected to Him, we can do anything. Nothing is impossible. We can beat the odds. If you believe God can use you, and you speak that out loud, then you will be used of God.

The Bible tells us to pray for everything—from the most seemingly insignificant concerns to the most life-impacting events. As you spend time with God, pray about and believe for everything, and you will get God's everything. Whether you are praying for the healing of a loved one with cancer, or seeking a good parking space on your day full of errands, you need to trust God for all of it. By doing this you are turning over every aspect of your life to Him, and your faith is being increased.

It is one thing to start saying the right things and start speaking God's Word. It is a whole different level of faith to completely stop speaking negative thoughts. Though we may want to be positive about the things we are believing God for, it can still be a challenge not to put some kind of limit or qualification on our dreams. Here's what I mean: It is no good to say, "I believe God will bless me with a new job," if you follow that up with "if it is still available." You aren't trusting that God will make a way, if you are looking for obstacles that might trip Him up, or if you hold your breath just in case, or if you're scared of getting your hopes up.

I read something the other day that said, "You are never stuck. You just keep re-creating the same experience over and over by thinking the same thoughts, maintaining the same beliefs, speaking the same words and doing the same things." Stop speaking negative things over your dreams. It's a form of complaining, and as you learned in the last chapter, complaining does nothing to change circumstances. You know where it got Pharaoh, and even the Israelites. It makes you stay where you are and have more of the same of what you're getting. You have to change the way you think and change the way you speak.

What Are You Affirming?

Earlier in the book, I shared with you the story of Jim Carrey, how he wrote his dreams on paper and used his words to create his dreams. He once told a reporter, "When I wasn't doing anything in Hollywood, I'd go up every night, sit on Mulholland Drive, look out at the city, stretch out my arms, and say 'Everybody wants to work with me. I'm a really good actor. I have all kinds of great movie offers.'" Carrey did this every night, not just once a year on January 1, or on his birthday. Every night he looked at the city where he wanted to work, and then he spoke his dreams. He would say out loud what he wanted as if it were already happening. "I would just repeat these things over and over and over, literally convincing myself that I had a couple of movies lined up. I'd drive down that hill ready to take the world on . . . It was like total affirmation."[2]

149

An affirmation is a statement that describes a goal in its already completed state or speaks of nonexistent things as if they already exist. In his book *The Success Principles*, Jack Canfield describes a good way to change your speech to line up with your dreams. He encourages people to start with the words "I am." He explains, "These are two of the most powerful words in the English language. . . . Your spirit or your subconscious mind takes any sentence that starts with 'I am' and interprets it as a command or a directive to make it happen."[3] For example, when you say, "I am enjoying feeling healthy in life, full of energy, at my perfect body weight of (whatever number you choose)," your spirit interprets that as a command that you will weigh that amount.

Canfield also said, "Use the present tense. Describe what you want as though you already have it, as though it is already accomplished." Instead of saying, "I am going to get a new red Porsche 911," Canfield says, "I am enjoying driving my new red Porsche 911." Instead of saying, "I will create my own line of clothing one day," say, "I am working hard at my clothing line company and enjoying every minute of it." Instead of saying, "I will open a soup kitchen to feed the homeless in my community," say, "I am praising God for the opportunity to serve others through my soup kitchen He is helping me build."[4] This is what it means to speak your dream as if it has already happened. Believe that you have received it, and it will be yours.

One more thing: Keep your words brief. Don't ramble on in your affirmation. Most of the time, excess verbiage is confusing and makes it harder to remember. Keep it short and simple so that it's memorable enough to easily recall when you're speaking these goals verbally.

Dig in Your Heels, Especially if You've Slipped Up

Let's talk about determination or, as I like to say, digging in your heels. What in the world does that mean? It means refusing to change your mind and not hesitating to take drastic action when necessary. I believe that God has given each of us a purpose. He has given us dreams He wants us to pursue during our time here on earth. He has given us a vision to achieve and goals to accomplish. But too many times we give up. We quit because of haunting fears from past failures; because of the baggage we carry with us from our past experiences; because it's too hard; because we get tired and unmotivated. The list of excuses is endless. All this negativity can only lead us to one place—quitting.

I want to talk to you about not giving up. Ever. Refuse to change your mind. Don't turn your back on the changes you want to see in your life. Dig in your heels no matter how it feels. Set your mind for success. Make up your mind to accomplish the dreams you have written for yourself. The Bible actually tells us not to grow weary in doing well (see Gal. 6:9). If you are working toward a dream that God has placed on your heart, you are "doing well," because God intends to bless you so that you can be a blessing to others in His name (see Gen. 12:2). You must find the courage and the strength to keep the momentum going. Refuse to change your mind. Refuse to be deterred from the path God has set you on.

Micah 7:8 says, "Do not gloat over me, my enemy, though I have fallen I will rise. Though I sit in darkness, the Lord will be my light." I can't say it enough—Satan is always on the prowl, trying to trip you up. He wants you down for the count. He wants you to give up and walk away. The devil doesn't want to see you pursuing your dreams. He is committed to keeping you from your success. His goal is to prevent you from trusting God, from believing that anything is possible with your life. He exists for the sole purpose of tricking us into a life of failure. He doesn't want us to pray or to have hope that something good can actually happen now or in our future.

151

Many times, we dwell on past failures to such an obsessive degree that we don't even try again. This is an area where Satan thrives. If he can convince us not to try, he doesn't have to lift another finger. He can sit back and watch us do nothing. As soon as we stop pursuing God's purpose for our life, Satan gets what he wants. He has prevented us from reaching others, from doing something to build the Kingdom and from living an abundant life with purpose and meaning. You cannot let him win that easily.

If you are in that discouraging place right now and have stopped dead in your tracks regarding your dreams, or you're on the verge of quitting, I want you to get up and start moving. Get out your dream book, spend time reviewing it and dig in your heels. Do not let your mind talk you out of doing something that you know you need to do.

Whether your dream is to lose weight, pay off your debts, write a book, sing a song, start a business, get married, have children, foster a child or build an orphanage, I want you to get serious about it. There is something about a made-up mind that brings results. When you press forward with the strength of your convictions, you will see your dreams fulfilled. I heard speaker and author Joyce Meyer say that her desire is to get people to understand that if they would make up their minds, they could overcome anything and do anything God tells them to do. Joyce said, "We can handle anything that life throws at us through Christ that strengthens us. We are not weak. We are warriors."

Maybe you know someone who needs to lose quite a bit of weight, and they've tried so many times and have been unsuccessful. They feel stuck and always say, "I just can't do it. I've tried every diet. It's hopeless." Then one day, they become determined that they don't want to be in bondage to the weight any longer. They're on a mission. You can tell from talking to them that their attitude is different. Their mindset has changed. They are committed to get their body in the best shape of their life, no matter how long it takes. That's what it means to dig in your heels and commit to your goals and dreams. When you make that decision, you know you've reached a turning point. It feels like every cell of your body is devoted to seeing your mission through, to making it a reality and enjoying the positive results when they come (and they will).

They *Never* Gave Up

153

When I read these stories, I was not only amazed by what these individuals overcame, but I also had to stop and ask myself, *What on earth do I have to complain about?* I hope these people will inspire you and give you hope for your own journey.

Dean Rhodes
Dean Rhodes was an American businessman who made some incredibly bad business decisions and opted out of buying into some of the most lucrative start-ups at ground level. Look at some of the opportunities he missed:

1. He was given the chance to invest in the fast-food chain Wendy's in the beginning, when he met a young Dave Thomas. He didn't do it.

2. Later, Rhodes met a man named Colonel Sanders and, at that time, he had an opportunity to buy stock in his company before it went national. He turned that down as well.

3. When Rhodes was in the restaurant equipment business, he met a man named Ray Kroc, who gave him the chance to invest in a little hamburger stand called McDonald's. Didn't happen.

4. A few years later, Rhodes was on a cruise when he met an attorney from the Pacific Northwest who suggested he invest in his son's new computer company, but it had a funny name: Microsoft. Rhodes declined.

By now you might be shaking your head in disbelief, wondering how he could live with these losses. Rhodes saw his mistakes for what they were and he continued to pursue his dreams and other opportunities. Eventually, he did find his success and saw his name at number 289 on the Forbes list of the 400 most successful business owners of America.[5]

Admiral Robert Peary

Admiral Robert Peary was a commander in the U.S. Navy. Over a period of 22 years, he made seven attempts to reach the North Pole. He covered miles and miles of the Arctic, suffering a number of injuries and illnesses from the harsh conditions. He also endured a lot of criticism from his peers, family and society in general. Finally, in 1908-1909, he made a last expedition, determined to reach the North Pole or die trying. He did reach his destination after fighting a harsh battle with brutal weather and without the benefit of modern technology.[6]

Oscar Hammerstein

Oscar Hammerstein, one of Broadway's most beloved and celebrated composers, had five flop shows that lasted less than six weeks combined before he wrote *Oklahoma!* In an industry where you are only as successful as your last project, Hammerstein refused to give up. He kept trying until he found the inspiration to create one of the most well-known musicals of our time. *Oklahoma!* ran for 269 weeks and grossed over $7 million. The show is still performed around the country on big stages and in community theatres.[7]

Albert Einstein, Edgar Allan Poe and John Shelley

These three individuals were all expelled from school for being what, in their time, was called "mentally slow." Albert Einstein was expelled from school because they thought he was dumb. Any one of these men could have accepted what their teachers and the school said about them and never aspired to do anything of significance, but they didn't accept it. They dreamed of more and refused to let anyone tell them they didn't have it in them. Not only did these great thinkers not give up, but they also didn't allow other people determine whether or not they succeeded.

155

Lawrence Hanratty

In 1995, Lawrence Hanratty was named the Unluckiest Man in New York. He was nearly electrocuted in a construction site accident in 1984, and stayed in a coma for weeks and was left permanently disabled. The disability claim he filed was delayed because he lost every lawyer, a total of four, who handled his case. The first one was disbarred, the next two died, and his wife ran off with the fourth. Later, Hanratty was hit by a careless driver and was robbed at the scene while waiting for the police. His insurance company tried to cut off his worker's compensation benefits, and his landlord threatened to kick him out of his apartment. Hanratty is dependent on oxygen and 42 different medications for heart and liver ailments that have been with him for years; but with help from neighbors and a state assemblyman, he is not giving up yet. Hanratty said of his experiences, "I say to myself, how much more am I going to be tested in life to see how much I can endure?" He concluded with a beautiful thought, "There's always hope."[8]

There have been times in my life when I thought I had it bad and felt sorry for myself. But I've learned something through those pity parties. I've learned that Satan has a way of magnifying our failures so that it's all we think about. He tries to amplify the things that aren't going right in our lives. He attempts to illuminate our frustrations and dissatisfactions. When we allow ourselves to focus on those negative thoughts, they multiply and overshadow our positive ones. If we keep concentrating on what is going wrong, we'll never see what is going right and, inevitably, we will want to give up.

Whether your dreams are to start a business, finish college, pass an important exam, become a mom, write a screenplay, teach illiterate adults how to read or become a missionary, letting your mistakes, failures or bad experiences become bigger than they are keeps you off the right path. Don't give up because you've had a setback or two. Don't let Satan play mind games on you. Don't listen to his lies that you are the only one who keeps failing and the only one who can't get it right.

Talk to anyone—a stranger on the street, a friend, a family member—or read someone's success story in a book or magazine and you will find that all of them have had at least one significant failure. Many people have had to overcome great odds and big obstacles but refused to give up their dream. In fact, President Theodore Roosevelt said, "The only man who never makes a mistake is the man who never does anything." He believed that life experience brings competence and helps us make fewer mistakes in the future.

If you feel as though your progress toward your dream is being tested, take heart, because you might be on the verge of a breakthrough. If you feel hopeless, defeated and discouraged, you've reached a critical juncture in your dream journey. It's the most important time to make up your mind, dig in your heels and stick to your guns. Do not give up on whatever it is God has put on your heart.

Live on Purpose and with Purpose

I read an African parable that said, "Every morning in Africa a gazelle wakes up. It knows that it must run faster than the fastest lion or it will be killed. Every morning a lion wakes up. It knows that it must outrun the slowest gazelle or it will starve to death. It doesn't matter whether you are the lion or you are the gazelle, when the sun comes up, you had better be running." I love this—*when the sun comes up, you had better be running*.

Too many dreams go unfulfilled, too many goals are never reached and too many visions never come to pass because we don't hit the ground running toward our dreams each day. Recently, I was researching the Internet for statistics on New Year's resolutions. I found an article that reported that 55 percent of American adults don't make any New Year's resolutions or goals. Another statistic suggested that 20 percent of New Year's goals are broken within the first week.[9] (Not the first month, but the first week. I couldn't believe it.)

If you've read any of my books or listened to any of my teachings on CD, YouTube or my website, you know that I love talking about goal setting. It's because goals are essential to keeping you alive. The enemy doesn't want you to reach your goals. Matter of fact, he'd prefer you not make any.

Satan is hoping that you do nothing significant. He wants to see you just exist—no changes, no progress, no growth, nothing. If you look at your life last year at this time, are you in the same place? If so, Satan is quite thrilled. That's exactly where he wants you to be. He wants you to stay the same, to stagnate, until the day you die. He has done his job if you didn't make any significant contributions and didn't fulfill the call of God on your life.

I hope that gets you as mad as it gets me! I want you to determine that this time next year, your life will be drastically different. You *will* see changes. You will have progressed. Make a commitment to do whatever is necessary to see that you have grown. Set the goal to accomplish more than you ever have in the past five years. Don't give up on your dreams. No matter how many times you've failed in the past, you are not a hopeless case. You have not made too many mistakes. You are not too far gone that God cannot reach down into the pit and pull you up. He wants to put you back on your feet and give you an assignment, a vision, a dream and goals to pursue.

I want you to refuse to change your mind when it comes to fulfilling the plan God has for your life. Make sure that on that day when you stand before God, you can tell Him you were faithful in what He had put in your heart and mind to do. Don't let anything or anyone take your focus off of your dreams, your vision and your goals. It's time to dig in your heels and live on purpose.

Make Up Your Mind

For some people, making a decision, whether big or small, is easy. For others, however, simply deciding what pair of shoes to wear can be a challenge. Here are some tips for making up your mind and sticking to it. These nuggets are useful in any area of your life, whether reaching for your dreams, accomplishing your goals, or making choices concerning your family, your career, or your ministry. They are pathways to learn how to dig in your heels in a practical way.

1. Decide What You Want

Look at the choice you have to make and the options available. Consider what you want, which of the options will accomplish that for you and settle on the one that comes closest to meeting your need without creating unnecessary complications.

2. Fix Your Mind on It

Once you have determined what you want, trust your instincts, God-given guidance and your decision-making ability. Believe that you have made the best decision based on the information you have, and move forward. Don't question yourself once you have settled on your path.

3. Write the Vision

Put your vision on paper and write out what you have decided to do about it. Physically seeing it will help you visualize it happening and see the road to success. It will also allow you to know what steps you have to take so you don't flounder around questioning your choices.

4. Educate Yourself

The ability to make an informed decision helps you feel confident about your choices. If you arm yourself with information and resources, you will have an easier time arriving at a decision that will make you feel secure. Do your homework. Dot the *Is*

159

and cross the *T*s. This way, you can answer any questions that try to keep you from setting out on a course of action.

5. Speak It Out of Your Mouth

Words have an immense amount of power. When we vocalize and verbalize our dreams and our desires, it gives them life. Words can lift us up or tear us down. Make the decision that you will use words for the good of your dreams, for the encouragement of others and for the acknowledgment of your life purpose.

6. Praise God Now

Don't wait. Show God how much you believe that He will do what He says He will do. Trust Him to make a way for the visions He has placed on your heart and the things He has put you here to accomplish. Thank Him for His wisdom, love, guidance and blessings; and do it in anticipation of these things rather than after you receive them.

7. Stop Being Led by Your Feelings

Because we are human, we are ruled by our emotions. They can bring positive experiences into our lives or destroy us. If we allow how we feel to interfere with what we know to be true, we are allowing the flesh to win. We are permitting Satan to take our focus off of God. Feelings are useful, but they should not influence our faith or guide us in our decisions.

Chapter 7

Express gratitude

*Be thankful for what you have and you will
end up having more. But if you concentrate on what you
don't have, you'll never, ever have enough.*
OPRAH WINFREY

· · · · ·

161

· · · · ·

Most people do not realize that focusing on what they do not have only causes them to attract never having it. When we find fault with and voice our complaints about our lives, we are actually creating an environment to receive more of what we are complaining about.

Remember, Proverbs 23:7 says that we are what we think in our hearts. What you think about, you continue to bring about. If you dwell on poverty, never having enough, always missing opportunities, never succeeding, always coming up short, then that is exactly what will come to you.

Someone once gave me a small book titled *212: The Extra Degree* by Sam Parker. In this quick read, I discovered that at 211 degrees, water is hot. At 212 degrees, it boils. Boiling water produces steam, and steam can actually power a locomotive. Raising the temperature of water by merely one degree means the difference between something being extremely hot and something generating enough force to power a massive machine.

One small change in your life could produce tremendous results. Using your mouth, expressing gratitude and voicing your thankfulness are that one small change that can catapult you from wishing to experiencing your dreams. I have tapped into that extra degree, and it has opened up a doorway of blessings, opportunities, favor and joy in my life like never before.

You have the ability to change the entire direction of your life with that little thing under your nose called your mouth. It's as simple as it seems. We read in Proverbs 18:21, "Death and life are in the power of the tongue, and they who indulge in it shall eat the fruit of it [for death or life]" (*AMP*). Every time you use speech, you speak life or death to your circumstances.

The *E* in IMAGINE BIG stands for "express gratitude." When you use your mouth to express gratitude for what you already have, you have just turned up the heat that one degree and opened the door for success. If you will adopt the discipline of voicing gratitude rather than complaints, you will experience greater success in seeing your dreams realized. Life coaches worldwide agree that being thankful even causes you to attract more to be thankful for.

Give God Thanks

The apostle Paul wrote, "Do not fret *or* have any anxiety about anything, but in every circumstance *and* in everything, by prayer and petition (definite requests), *with thanksgiving,* continue to make your wants known to God" (Phil. 4:6-8, *AMP,* emphasis added). Those two little words—*with thanksgiving*—have great significance. It is one thing to write your vision (or petition) on paper; it's another thing to thank God for its fulfillment.

When I was made aware of the importance of expressing gratitude, I realized that I needed to change some things in my life if my circumstances were to change. A new house was at the forefront of my mind. Rodney and I had to come up with a certain (large) amount of money to close on our new house— money we didn't have. I prayed, had faith and thanked God in advance. But I'll admit, I felt ridiculous the first few times I walked around my kitchen thanking Him for the deposit when clearly we didn't have the money. But the more I declared it out loud, the more I began to believe we would have it soon. What you repeatedly hear, you eventually believe. And what seemed impossible, at first, came to pass.

When you thank God for something that hasn't manifested yet, you are demonstrating the greatest faith. We read in Hebrews 11:6 that it is impossible to please God without faith. When you open your mouth and express gratitude to Him for something that hasn't even appeared yet, you are pleasing God.

I've noticed that wealthy and successful people are proactive. They do not wait to see what happens with life; they voice their dreams. They act as if their desires are happening. And they give thanks to God *before* their dreams are realized. Unsuccessful people just wait to see how life unfolds, complaining along the way and expecting nothing. They seem to get exactly what they expect. Take note of that pattern.

Use a proactive approach to your dreams. Voice your gratitude to God for what He is about to do in your life. Create an environment in your home, your car or your office that invites the presence of God by offering Him thanksgiving. I have chosen to make this practice a part of my daily life. I can't think of a day that goes by without expressing gratitude to God for what He's already done and for what He is about to do. When I do this, I truly "act as if" my dreams have already materialized.

In May 2011, I was speaking at a conference in North Carolina with Nancy Alcorn, my great friend, mentor and founder of Mercy Ministries. At the end of my session, I went to the green room to rest and connect with Nancy before lunch. As soon as I walked in the room, she blurted out, "Terri, you have got to meet some of my friends!"

"Sure," I replied. "Who are they?"

"They're the hosts of a success and motivational seminar where 15,000 people attend." She paused for a moment and said, "You are exactly the kind of speaker they would want at their event!"

As I heard Nancy's words, I felt a tremendous desire rise up in me to speak at that event. I also felt a sense of confirmation that it would happen. I didn't know how or when, but I knew it was something God had given me a desire to do. It was a God-inspired dream.

After I flew home to Texas, I went online to research that particular conference and found images of the event. I printed them out and placed one picture in my dreams and goals notebook and one on my vision board. Beside them I wrote, "I am so grateful to be a guest speaker at this conference in 2012 and beyond . . . in Jesus' name!" I even blocked off my calendar for the week the conference was scheduled and did not accept any invitations to speak. I also invested in this dream by giving away a thousand dollars. I believed God would manifest my desires.

Every day I would lift up this dream to the Lord and thank Him for its fulfillment. I did this *daily*. I was expecting my dream to be fulfilled. I should tell you that when I give thanks to God, it's not a quiet and reserved Heavenly-Father-I-thankest-Thee moment. I express the same emotion—the same squeals in my voice, the tightening of my fists, the jumping, smiling and ex-hilarating feelings of overwhelming appreciation—as if God has already brought my petitions to pass.

There were many times I would drive home from work bubbling with excitement and saying, "Thank You sooooo much, Jesus, that I AM a guest speaker at this conference! I am sooooo grateful! Thank You! Thank You! Thank You!" I would giggle as if I had just been handed the invitation. Let me tell you something: God responds to that kind of faith. When you eliminate doubt, unbelief and "How will this ever happen" questions, you are operating in faith. And you must have faith in your dreams if they are ever going to materialize.

Let's revisit Philippians 4:6: "Do not fret or have any anxiety about anything" (*AMP*). No anxiety? Really? About anything? When fear or worry starts to invade your mind and you do not see any positive signs that your dream will ever come to pass, read this Scripture out loud with assurance, boldness and faith.

Months went by after my conversation with Nancy. I had no indication that this dream would ever happen. But I didn't give up. I continued visualizing my dream and thanking God for it. Eleven months later, I was officially invited to be the guest speaker at that very motivational seminar attended by 15,000 businessmen and businesswomen (exactly the way I en-visioned it)!

God is faithful to His Word. He just wants you to believe it. Don't worry about anything. Trust God for the desires He has placed in your heart. Believe in Him to make a way where there seems to be no way. And thank Him ahead of time for making it happen.

There is no power in rehearsing facts. But there is power when you release your faith for the impossible. How? By ex-pressing gratitude now. For how long? Until you see your

165

dream come to pass (and then you praise God for it and thank Him for more dreams to come).

When Your Mouth Is Part of the Problem

After their exodus from Egypt and slavery, the Israelites circled the same mountain for 40 years. The journey should have taken no more than 11 days. Why the delay? Mainly, because of their mouths. They kept complaining about how bad their new life was: *We don't like it here. We're hungry. We're tired. We wish we were somewhere else. We'd rather be back in Egypt as slaves.* Their complaining kept them right where they were—in the desert.

Complaining will keep you in the same state—in bondage—for the rest of your life. God isn't moved by complaints; He is moved by faith. If you start praising and thanking Him ahead of time, you automatically act on your dreams and your goals by having an attitude of gratitude.

Several of the dreams I have recorded in my dream book have not come to fruition yet, but I thank God for them anyway. I give Him praise that they are happening. I am aware that my dreams will come to life when the time is right. Even if I don't see it, He is making a way. I am so grateful for what God has planned for me that I don't have to see it happening to know He is moving on my behalf.

A certain tribe in Asia puts the following curse on their enemies: "May you stay in one place for the rest of your life." That may not seem very evil as far as curses go, but can you imagine what that could actually mean in your life? *May you stay right where you are forever.* You will never grow. You will never improve your situation. You will never deepen your relationships.

When you complain, you are speaking a curse over yourself to stay right where you are. If you complain that you will never

166

lose weight, you never will lose weight. If you gripe that you never will get a better job, you will never get a better job. If you announce you will never find a good husband, you will never find a good husband. You have to change the way you talk. You have to control your mouth so that it doesn't lead you into another form of procrastination—stagnation.

Don't Worry, Just Worship

The shortest distance between you and God is when you praise and thank Him, especially as it concerns your dreams and what you believe Him to bring to your life. When you honor Him in this way, you express the greatest faith. Take some time now and thank God for the dreams that are coming to pass. Close your eyes and say, "Father, thank You. I don't know how my vision, my dreams and my goals are going to happen. I don't know when they're going to happen. I don't know how You're going to do it, but I thank You for it. Thank You for giving me the desires of my heart. Thank You for doing what seems impossible."

167

How did that make you feel? Did it inspire you? Did it make you stronger? Did you feel silly or awkward? When you give God thanks out loud, especially if your circumstances don't evidence the fruit of your dreams, you may feel a little nutty. But that's okay. You are releasing powerful faith. God loves when you do that. He rewards that kind of bold, steadfast and unshakable belief. The Bible tells us it's impossible to please God without faith (see Heb. 11:6). God wants to see faith evidence in your life. It shows that you trust Him fully, and it's when He can work most effectively in your life.

You won't ignite your faith and make your dreams reality only by reviewing them on paper. You have to activate your faith. You have to believe. You have to allow the truth of what your dream means to sink in and move you when you read it. Let it get deep down on the inside of you. Believe for it. Declare it with boldness, and thank God for it.

As I have illustrated, I have many dreams that I've written down on paper, and when I read them aloud, I act as if somebody just handed me the very thing I'm imagining. There are times when I'm in my guest bedroom with my dream book, reading it over and speaking my words out loud. Sure, sometimes I feel silly doing it. But who cares? There have been times when I've even jumped up and down and shouted my praises to God. Why should I feel self-conscious or embarrassed?

If somebody handed you a thousand dollars for you to keep, how would you respond? Would you quietly thank the person, not even looking into his eyes? Would you appreciate the gesture without any sign of emotion? Of course not! You'd probably go nuts. If you're like me, you would yell at the top of your lungs, "Thank You, Jesus! Thank You! Thank You! Thank You!" Admit it. You would! You might even dance. You might even drop to your knees.

Sometimes I do that when I'm meditating on my dream book in private with God. I will say to Him, "Father God, I praise You and thank You. Thank You so much for giving me the very desires of my heart. You are so faithful. You are so incredible. I thank You and praise You from my heart for giving me these things. You said if I would delight myself in You, You would give me the desires of my heart. Thank You for giving them to me." Doesn't my prayer sound like I have already received my dream? That is faith, pure and simple. When you praise and thank God, you are activating your faith and doing exactly what God's Word tells you to do.

Consider the example of Paul and Silas (read Acts 16:16-40). When they were in prison and began boldly and loudly worshiping God for His faithfulness, proclaiming how awesome and powerful He is, they were still shackled to the wall of a jail cell. They had been arrested. They had been beaten. They were bruised, battered and in pain. They were imprisoned with no visible hope of ever getting out. But their faith-filled words put God on the move. He sent an earthquake from heaven that shook the building. The walls began to crumble, the prison doors opened up, the chains fell off of them and they walked out of there free as could be. This supernatural event would never have happened had these two men of God not spoken their faith out loud. They had to give voice to their belief in and devotion to God. Your life will never change until you begin vocalizing what you believe God intends to do for you and through you.

169

The Power of Praise

What comes out of your mouth is vitally linked to whether or not you have victory. Your words, when spoken, can be a powerful weapon against the enemy or they can doom you to failure. Words of praise and thanksgiving are devastating to the devil. When you speak (or sing) in this manner, it can speak life to yourself and death to his plan of destruction. This is what motivates me to ignite my faith by worshiping God.

Praising God Drives the Devil Crazy

When I think how desperately Satan is trying to stop me from pursuing my dreams and goals, it makes me want to fight back. He's the one who wants to keep me stagnant and discouraged by trying to wedge a foothold of doubt into my life. He's the one who tries to drag me down and get me to give up on what I am here to do. And I can't stand it! So how do I get him back? How do I make him pay for what he's done to me? By praising, worshiping and thanking God. These are weapons of mass destruction that drive the devil crazy. When you take time to sing praises, it confuses Satan. Your efforts to lift up the Lord are an aggressive means to attack him. And it works!

Praise Helps You Give God Control
Here's what else praising God will do—it solidifies your commitment to fully surrender yourself to God. When you finally give God your all, He takes control. He is waiting for you to put your complete trust in Him, especially as it concerns your vision, dreams and goals. Matthew 33:6 says, "Seek ye first the kingdom of God and his righteousness and all these things shall be added unto you" (*KJV*). Note that the Scripture says *all* these things, not some of them or one thing—"all these things" will be yours. I want you to understand that as you seek God, as you spend time with Him, and as you worship Him, you are making an investment in your future. You are trusting that He has already done what you are believing Him for. Doing this will open the door for God to begin moving in your life.

Praise Is an Atmosphere in Which God Works
Worship creates an atmosphere where God begins to work. Remember, the Bible is full of stories of people bowing down and worshiping God before they got their breakthrough. Worship Him first and foremost on your journey to fulfill your vision. Don't thank Him after your dreams come true and you reach your goals. Sure, it's easy to thank somebody after they've done something nice for you. But worshiping God before you see results shows Him that you wholeheartedly believe in the vision He has given you and that you are going to give it everything you've got.

You may have tried this in the past and gotten discouraged. You may be thinking, *Terri, I have been worshiping God that I'm free from debt, that my bills are paid and that I have money in the bank, but nothing has changed.* I know it might be hard and it requires a lot of faith, especially when the natural dictates the opposite of what you believe; but you've got to do it. And you've got to keep doing it.

If you are on the verge of giving up right now, be encouraged that you are close to victory. You are close to your dream. My dad believes that feeling as if you have no choice but to quit is always an indication that your breakthrough is right around the corner. Don't give up. Determine in your heart that no matter how impossible your dreams may look at this very moment, you will hang in there.

Paul wrote, "For in due season we shall reap, *if we faint not*" (Gal. 6:9, *KJV*, emphasis added). Persevering when things get tough is a long-term commitment. You don't try to dig in your heels to see how it goes. You can't treat it like a test run; if you don't get results immediately, you go back to your old ways. You must determine that you will not quit. You will not give up.

You will faint not, and reap your dreams.

What Are You Thankful For?

My dad says, "The depth of your praise determines the magnitude of your breakthrough." Being grateful is a habit you must practice regularly. I want you to get into the routine of thanking God for anything and everything. Right now, take some time and think of about 20 things for which you are grateful. Include things you are enjoying right now and dreams and desires that have not yet come to pass. When you are done making your list, tell God out loud how thankful

171

you are for His past, present and future provisions and manifestations in your life.

1. _____
2. _____
3. _____
4. _____
5. _____
6. _____
7. _____
8. _____
9. _____
10. _____
11. _____
12. _____
13. _____
14. _____
15. _____
16. _____
17. _____
18. _____
19. _____
20. _____

Chapter 8

BE LED BY YOUR GOD-GIVEN DESIRES

Focus more on your desire than on your doubt,
and the dream will take care of itself . . . Your doubts are not as
powerful as your desires, unless you make them so.
MARCIA WIEDER

"How do I know if my dreams and visions are God's plans for my life?"

I hear that question frequently. I've even asked it myself when stretching my imagination to believe for great things. I would think, *Am I just making this stuff up? What if I pursue something that isn't what God wants me to do with my life? How can this be God if it's something I enjoy and desire? Am I being selfish by following the desires of my heart?* Do any of those thoughts sound familiar to you?

Here's what I've discovered. When you regularly spend time with God, He will begin to show you things to come. You will start seeing a flash of your future, a preview of what God is about to do in your life. This process produces desire. Your imagination will begin to rouse in you desire for particular dreams.

The truth that I'm about to share with you has the power to radically change your life and ignite in you a flame to produce momentum that will take you right to your dream. Are you ready? *God supernaturally orders your steps by the desires of your heart!*

Our Desires, God's Desires

The *B* in *IMAGINE BIG* stands for "Be led by your God-given desires." I believe that many times we get the idea that our dreams are totally unrelated to the desires of our heart. But that isn't true. When God communicates direction to your life, it comes to you as an idea in your imagination, and it's always connected to desire.

The Word says, "Delight yourself also in the LORD, and He shall give you the desires of your heart" (Ps. 37:4, *NKJV*). I had always interpreted that verse to mean that God will give me whatever I want, but only if I delight myself in Him. While that's true, I felt God moving me to think of this passage another way. If we delight ourselves in the Lord, He is the one who gives us the desires that are in our hearts.

In other words, if you are delighting yourself in the Lord, God is the one who gave you that desire to be extremely wealthy. He wants to bless you so that you will be a blessing in His name, as He promised Abraham in Genesis 12:2: "I will bless you . . . and you will be a blessing" (*NKJV*). God gave you that desire to be a best-selling author. God gave you that desire to have a television show that reaches millions of people. God gave you that desire to open a daycare center. God gave you that desire to fly corporate jets. God gave you that desire to produce movies. God gave you that desire to be the top salesman at a Fortune 500 company. God gave you that desire to record music.

You didn't just make up your dreams. And you're not being selfish by having those desires. God gives you these things as you continue to spend time with Him. He supernaturally plants unique dreams and desires on your heart for you to pursue as you partner with Him.

Here's the cool part—the desires we have are purposed to order our steps. Psalm 37:5 continues, "Commit your way unto the LORD, trust also in Him, and He shall bring it to pass" (*NKJV*). What is the "it" that the psalmist refers to? It's the desire God has given you. If you didn't have a desire, you couldn't commit your way unto the Lord. You wouldn't even know how to go about doing it.

I learned from Pastor Mac Hammond that God reveals "the way" by the desire of your heart, and you commit your way by following the desire of your heart. He says, "When you commit your way unto the Lord (and that means allowing the desires of your heart to order your steps, trusting in God, and trusting in those desires), He will bring them to pass!"

We read, "The steps of a good man are ordered by the LORD" (Ps. 37:23, *NKJV*). How does the Bible define a "good man"? A good man (or woman) is one who delights in God's way, the way that's revealed by the desire of his (or her) heart. Remember, if you are delighting in God, He is giving you the desires of your heart, and they will be what is in God's heart for you. There's no room for selfish desires here. The message of this Scripture, and verse 4 of that same chapter, is that when we follow the desire of our hearts, our steps are ordered.

A caveat: A quick and easy measuring tool to determine if your desire is from God or from your own selfish motive is to spend time examining it. Ask God to help you do this. If you can honestly say that your desire is for the purpose of fulfilling the call of God and being a blessing to those around you, then you can trust it's from Him. The more time you spend with God and in His Word, the clearer your desires will become and the more intense you will be about pursuing them.

• • • • •

175

• • • • •

I promise that as you keep your desires in check, He will remove from your life the ones that are not from Him.

You will probably not know all the steps to take each day to achieve your dreams, but as you fill your mind consistently with the images of what you desire, God will supernaturally order your steps to make that dream happen. Every day will move you closer to the divine plan God has for your life.

As I've already mentioned, the desires of your heart are dependent upon you "delighting" yourself in the Lord. We read in Psalm 1:1-3:

> Blessed (happy, fortunate, prosperous, and enviable) is the man who walks and lives not in the counsel of the ungodly [following their advice, their plans and purposes], nor stands [submissive and inactive] in the path where sinners walk, nor sits down [to relax and rest] where the scornful [and the mockers] gather. But his delight and desire are in the law of the Lord, and on His law (the precepts, the instructions, the teachings of God) he habitually meditates (ponders and studies) by day and by night. And he shall be like a tree firmly planted [and tended] by the streams of water, ready to bring forth its fruit in its season; its leaf also shall not fade or wither; and everything he does shall prosper [and come to maturity] (*AMP*).

This Scripture tells us that the person who delights in the Lord, who meditates on His Word, who is pursuing and walking out God's plan for his or her life (which includes imagining dreams and goals) will experience prosperity. Remember the words of Genesis 11:6. Whatever you imagine to do will not be restrained from you. Desire and imagination work hand in hand to produce God's direction for your life. The more you think about, meditate on and imagine living out your dreams, the bigger those desires will grow and expand. It will create in you a determination to see them come to pass.

How Badly Do You Want It?

I believe the number-one motivating factor behind the achievement of your dreams is intense desire. How badly you desire to see a dream manifested dictates your behavior and reflects the level of effort you are willing to make. If you desire something intensely, you'll get it.

Desire is the first push to change. The things you *really* want influence the amount of work, persistence and commitment you're willing to put forth. Your best effort will be spent in the areas where you have the greatest desires. The truth is . . .

177

If you really want to lose weight, you will.

If you really want to get out of debt, you will.

If you really want to start a new business, you will.

If you really want to go on that European cruise, you will.

If you really want to write a book, you will.

If you really want to draw closer to God, you will.

It's simple. We do what we really want to do. If a guy really wants to go out with a girl, he will call. He will text. He will show up. He will do all these things because he wants to. Because he desires this girl. If he doesn't, he won't call. He won't text. He won't show up.

Desire is what will bring about change in your life. You are where you are this minute because of yourself—because of the extent of your desires, and how badly (or not) you want something. In the past, I've made financial goals. Some I had even written down and prayed over. But, like my New Year's goals,

I would put them in a drawer somewhere and never think about them again. The result? Nothing. I remained in debt. I was still paying my monthly bills even though I wanted to be debt free.

I've had other financial goals that I was serious about and committed to reaching, no matter how impossible they appeared. I wrote down those goals, prayed over them and kept them in front of me continually—confessing, believing God and sowing seed for them. I had a burning desire to accomplish my dreams, and nothing was going to stop me. I made sacrifices. I dug in my heels. I was willing to do what it took to see those dreams fulfilled—and they were.

True desire is manifested in your results. If you're getting the same results, you're probably doing the same thing you've always done (and whatever it is, it's not bringing you closer to your dreams). Weak desires bring weak results. Your desire to see your dreams fulfilled cannot be a hope or a wish. It must be a definite intention on the inside of you that exceeds anything else.

How *True* Are Your *Intentions?*

I was reading the book *If How To's Were Enough, We'd All be Skinny, Rich and Happy.* The message was that your true intentions equal your results. Many of us want to do things, but there is a big difference between wanting and having a true intention.

The author compares wanting something versus having a true intention this way. If you set a goal of earning $100,000 but only earn $70,000, your goal was not your true intention.

It doesn't mean you didn't want to earn $100,000, but your so-called intention was more like a wish. It wasn't a solid commitment. It wasn't a deep focus. It wasn't a true intention.

Think about your vision. Think about your dreams. Think about your goals. Think about your desires. Are you committed to them? Are you willing to do the hard work? Are you willing to give up certain things to live them out? Are you willing to be disciplined to be debt free, to lose weight, to deepen your relationship with God, to build your dream house, to finish school? If so, chances are your desires, your true intentions, will become realities.

179

Deepen Your Desires

I'm convinced that the amount of time it takes to bring to pass what you are imagining depends upon the intensity and momentum behind your desire. In order to develop deep desires, you have to change the focus of your attention. For example, stop looking at what you're giving up in the process of reaching your dream and focus on where you're going. Stop focusing on the food you shouldn't be eating and start focusing on the image of your body at your ideal weight. The more you focus on your desire and all it will entail, the deeper you will desire it. And the deeper you desire it, the more you will do what it takes to achieve that goal.

You might be saying in response, "Terri, I really desire to lose weight, but I'm not losing any." That statement reveals that you likely have a *competing desire*: food. You may have a stronger desire to indulge in sugary snacks than to get healthy and drop some weight (unless, of course, you have a medical or health-related reason that needs to be evaluated by a doctor). You have to eliminate your competing desire by focusing on your true intention.

How badly do you desire to build your savings account? If your desire to shop for new clothes is greater than your desire to save money, then you'll stay in debt. If you spend most of your time looking at the latest clothing catalogs or fashion magazines, you'll never change your desire. You have to re-route your focus. Change the direction of your mind. Start reading books about financial freedom until your desire to save money burns on the inside of you, and you are giving full attention to being debt free and financially secure.

Joshua 1:8 tells us, "Never stop reading this Scroll of the Law. Day and night you must think about what it says. Make sure you do everything that is written in it. Then things will go well with you. And you will have great success" (*NIRV*). You may not automatically have a love for reading God's Word or listening to faith-building messages or even spending time in prayer; but as you start giving these things your attention, eventually a desire will grow to do them. Warning: Don't quit because you don't see change automatically. You have to stay grounded in faith that change will come.

When Fear Overwhelms Desire

Fear is the number-one enemy to your success. It will rob you of your dreams. Satan uses your fears to fuel his attacks. He does not want you to fulfill the plan God has for your life. He does not want you to pursue the dreams God has put in your heart. He will intimidate you at whatever cost so that you give up.

One definition of fear is to run away from something. What are you running from in your life because of fear? Is it your calling? A new line of work? An audition or an interview? A speaking engagement? A bank loan for a business idea? Sometimes you need to just do it. Say yes and dive in to what you feel God is leading you to do.

One summer, I was at the lake with my family. We were taking turns jumping off the boathouse into the water, about a 15-foot plunge from the roof to the water. My nephew Preston, who was about seven at the time, couldn't take his eyes off of his big brother and Uncle Rodney repeatedly jumping off the top. Finally, Preston got up the nerve to climb up on the roof. That's as far as he got. He inched his way to the edge, and then started backing up as soon as his feet hit the ledge.

We tried to encourage him and yelled, "Jump, Preston! You can do it!" I could see his little knees shaking as he stretched his neck out over the edge and looked at the distance to the water. Finally, Preston sat down. He wanted off the roof. After what seemed like an hour of watching him contemplate this decision, Rodney picked him up and dropped him into the water. Preston screamed the whole way down. I think I did, too. I felt so bad for the little guy.

The minute his head bobbled up to the surface, Preston broke out in a wide grin and shouted, "That was fun!" Next thing I knew, Preston had climbed onto the boathouse and ran up to the top, ready for his second jump.

Don't let fear stop you from jumping all the way into what God has for your life. Don't allow fear to prevent you from doing what you know God is telling you to do. Don't allow fear to keep you from accomplishing great things. Here is one of my favorite Scriptures:

Fear not [there is nothing to fear], for I am with you;
do not look around you in terror and be dismayed, for

181

I am your God. I will strengthen and harden you to difficulties, yes, I will help you; yes, I will hold you up and retain you with My [victorious] right hand of rightness and justice (Isa. 41:101, *AMP*).

I want you to grab hold of the first seven words of this passage: "Fear not [there is nothing to fear]." "Nothing" means nothing. Because of all the fears I dealt with in my life, I hung that Bible verse on a wall in my office as a reminder. You have absolutely nothing to fear as long as you believe God is with you. No matter how tough things get. No matter how far away your dream. No matter how impossible your desire. You don't have to be afraid.

Satan works through fear just like God works through faith. When you fear, you activate Satan's power in your life. When you have faith, you activate God's power in your life. This is why it's so important to build your faith. Don't let fear stand in the way of your vision, dreams, goals and desires. You can overcome your fears by meditating on and staying in God's Word. Do something every day to build your faith and intensify your God-given desires so that they alter your behavior to pursue your dreams with passion, commitment and steadfastness.

Former diplomat and recipient of the Presidential Medal of Freedom Robert Strauss said, "Success is a little like wrestling a gorilla. You don't quit when you're tired—you quit when the gorilla is tired."

Don't ever give up until you see your desires fulfilled.

Fear Versus Faith

As you take steps to see your dreams actualized, it's important to study the Bible. It will help you stay focused on what

God is calling you to do. It will deepen your desires. It will help you determine the difference between which dreams are from Him and which come from selfish ambition. Studying His Word will also help you increase your faith and decrease your fears. As I've said, fear is the number-one deterrent from your dreams and desires coming to pass.

Look up the following Scriptures and meditate on them: 1 Chronicles 5:20, Psalm 62:8, Isaiah 50:10, Daniel 6:23, John 14:1 and Hebrews 10:23. Let God speak to your heart through them. Allow these words to penetrate your mind. Let them fill your spirit with faith and diminish any fears you may have of pursuing what God is calling you to do or be.

* * * * *

183

* * * * *

Chapter 9

INVEST IN YOUR DREAMS

It is one of the beautiful compensations of this life that no man can sincerely try to help another without helping himself.
RALPH WALDO EMERSON

When you bless someone or invest your money into someone else's dream, you help yourself more than you help him or her. You strategically put yourself in a position to receive from God. Isn't that exciting?

A couple of months ago, I was given $200 for my birthday. I could hardly wait to go to the mall and get some beautiful new tops I saw there the week before. The shirts were gorgeous. One was aqua blue with rhinestones. Another was pink with tie-dye swirls of blue and green. I could just picture myself wearing them.

On my way to the mall, I received a text message from a friend who asked me to pray for her. The brakes on her car went out and she had no money to get them repaired. I prayed for her and hung up the phone. I needed to make a decision. Should I buy the tops or give the money to my friend? Which choice would put me in a better position financially? Obviously, give! I didn't have to think twice. I could hardly wait to text her back and say, "Don't worry about it. Consider your brakes paid!"

When you're able to be a blessing to someone in need, it's the greatest feeling in the world. A blessing is defined as "an instrument through which God's divine favor flows, bringing peace, joy and contentment and preventing misfortune in the life of another."

Did you know that when you give, you are most like God? John 3:16, one of the most famous verses in the Bible, says, "For God so loved the world that He gave." When we love, we give. And when we give, we represent the image of God.

Kassidi has certain characteristics that are like me and some that are exactly like her daddy. My husband is quite the prankster. He is constantly trying to make me laugh. In fact, when the pizza man comes to our front door, Rodney always makes me go get it. Meanwhile, he's in the background yelling in a dramatic, country Texas accent, "Baby, I'm hone-gryyyyy! Hurry up! Get me some pizzzzzaaa!" (The delivery guy thinks we're nuts, but I like to think of ourselves as entertaining.) I used to be embarrassed at Rodney's antics, but I'm used to them now. Even my daughter chimes in with him. That's when I tell her, "You are acting just like your dad."

Well, don't you know that you are just like your heavenly father? God is a giver, and He made you one too.

I've been told that the greatest level of contentment and satisfaction comes about when we find a way to serve others. Jesus measured greatness in terms of service, not our status. Rick Warren, in his best-selling book *The Purpose Driven Life*, says, "God determines your greatness by how many people you serve, not how many people serve you."[1] Jesus said, "Whoever wants to be great must become a servant" (Mark 10:43, *THE MESSAGE*). These messages are totally contrary to the way our world operates. But God works in a totally different system than the world. When we give, we receive. We become a blessing. We plant seed for our dream to harvest.

The last *I* in *IMAGINE BIG* stands for "invest in your dreams." I'm going to show you how being a blessing to others helps to determine your destiny. How giving, especially when we don't have much to offer, blesses us greatly. I want you to get a proper perspective about having money and giving money. God wants you to be blessed and successful so you can be a blessing to others. The apostle Paul wrote, "Be mindful to be a blessing" (Gal. 6:10, *AMP*). Being blessed means being empowered to prosper.

God doesn't want you to view giving as a religious obligation. It is a choice you make simply because you love Him and want to honor Him with your finances. Giving, by the way, is also evidence of our gratitude toward God and everything He gives us. Paul's words teach us, "Let each one [give] as he has made up his own mind *and* purposed in his heart, not reluctantly *or* sorrowfully or under compulsion, for God loves (He takes pleasure in, prizes above other things, and is unwilling to abandon or to do without) a cheerful (joyous, "prompt to do it") giver [whose heart is in his giving]" (2 Cor. 9:7, *AMP*). I love how *THE MESSAGE* translates this verse:

> Remember: A stingy planter gets a stingy crop; a lavish planter gets a lavish crop. I want each of you to take plenty of time to think it over, and make up your own mind what you will give. That will protect you against sob stories and arm-twisting. God loves it when the giver delights in the giving.

God honors a giving heart. Interestingly enough, my organization has been more blessed financially this year than

. . . . .
187
. . . . .

ever before. At the same time, we have also given more finances and resources this year than in prior years. We have purposely looked for areas to give big.

Your Giving Will Determine Your Destiny

The book of Genesis reveals that God has given to each of us two gifts—authority (dominion) and seed. Sowing seed and reaping harvest is a natural and spiritual law that is recorded in Genesis 8:22. We have the ability to determine our own destiny by the seeds we sow. I love what my dad says, "You may not have what you need but you're never without the seed that will produce it."

Seed represents your future. When you plant a garden, you know what you're sowing. You don't just throw the seeds out on the soil and wonder what you've planted. The seeds come in their own packages and there's even a picture on them that tells you what the seed will produce. This is your vision. As it concerns your dreams, you should never toss money in an offering plate at church or donate to a charity without being specific about what you're sowing toward. "A man's harvest in life depends entirely upon the seeds that he sows" (Gal. 6:7, *Phillips*). Know what harvest you expect to produce. Know what dreams, goals and desires you want fulfilled.

You must give in order to receive more. I understand how foolish it might seem to give, especially when you have financial burdens. However, I have lived out this principle in my life so many times that no one can convince me it doesn't work. In chapter 7, I briefly mentioned the down payment Rodney and I needed for a new house. Here's what happened. Years ago, we were getting ready to build our second home. I was four months pregnant and eager to move into a bigger house. We had one snag. In order to reduce the monthly payment to an amount we could afford at that time, we needed to come up with $48,000 as our initial down payment.

I vividly remember Rodney and me sitting in the builder's office when we were given that information. We both swallowed real hard and said, "Okay, we'll have the $48,000 by the deadline." While we expressed confidence in our gutsy declaration, the truth was that our current financial situation looked dismal. We were living paycheck to paycheck and had only $1,000 in our savings account. Also, our move-in date was January 30, 1997, just five months away. How in the world could we come up with $48,000 in that shortness of time?

After that surreal moment in the builder's office, Rodney and I went home and took a long, hard look at our finances. We recognized that all we had was $1,000, but we also realized that it was the best we had. My dad's words rose in my spirit and replayed in my head over and over: "You may not have what you *need* but you are never without the *seed* that will produce it."

Rodney and I both agreed that what we had was nowhere near enough to meet our need, so we decided to turn it into significant seed. We gave all of it away. We sowed the best seed we had. A thousand dollars may not seem like much to you, but to us at the time, it was significant. We had faith that our investment would reap a reward. Like Mike Murdock says, our seed was a photograph of our faith.

After Rodney and I invested into our future by giving, we took a picture of the blueprints of our dream home and taped it to our refrigerator door. I kept a copy on my desk at work as well. Underneath the picture I wrote, "Thank You, Jesus, for $48,000 by January 30, 1997." I also listed this dollar amount in increments of a thousand dollars until the figure came to zero, where I penned, "Paid in Full." Rodney and I daily kept that vision before our eyes. I had faith that I would soon be crossing off the $1,000 increments one by one. We also contin-uously exercised our faith by thanking the Lord for the mani-festation of our dream on time. We believed that we would have the money somehow, some way. We had no idea how God would bring it about, but we just knew He would.

I have discovered that the number-one question that will stop you from achieving your dreams is asking "How?" My advice to you? Don't ask. Just believe. Your job is not to figure out how your dreams will manifest. Your responsibility is to stay focused on the vision, sow seed toward it and trust God to bring it about. Don't get bogged down by the particulars of His plan to actual-ize the impossible. Keep imagining, keep reviewing, keep pray-ing; and in a matter of time, He'll reveal ideas, opportunities, resources and relationships to make your dream come true.

That's exactly what happened in our situation. God uncovered opportunities for Rodney and me to make money. We did every-thing from selling pinball machines we found at a garage sale to ghostwriting books for other authors. Rodney went door to door in our neighborhood painting address numbers on the curbs out-side people's homes. I taught French to little children after school. We seized every chance we had to make money, and God continued to bring opportunities to us. We rejoiced every time we were able to mark off another thousand dollars on our written vision.

When we had six weeks to go and still needed $20,000, yes, our situation looked a little frightening. We continued to proac-tively look for opportunities to work, make extra money and dili-gently pursue this vision with intense desire. The day finally came when we were scheduled to meet with the bank to prove that we had the amount needed to close on our new home. We showed up with $38,600, not the $48,000 we were told we needed. As we sat in the bank sweating a little bit, the loan officer punched in some numbers on his computer. Finally, he said, "After reviewing everything, it appears that your home has come under budget and the down payment needed to move in is $38,000."

We had more than enough! God is ever faithful. Rodney and I were able to raise $38,600 in only a few months when previously we had saved only $1,000 in five years. What was the difference? Vision. Taking Action. Desire. Faith. Giving.

The Amount Doesn't Matter; It's the Seed that Counts

Invest in your dreams by sowing. Sow a financial seed. Sow your time. Sow your resources. Sow what you have. Sow your best. Recently, I cleaned out my closet and collected five trash bags full of clothes to give away. Not junk. Nice clothes, some of which I had never even worn. I gave them to some ladies I work with and some of my co-workers' spouses. Within a month, I received a $350 gift card to my favorite store, another gift card to Macy's, one to Dillard's, and $200 cash! I'm reminded of what the apostle Paul wrote: "Whoever sows sparingly will also reap sparingly, and whoever sows generously will also reap generously" (2 Cor. 9:6).

191

Seeds I've Sown for
My Personal Vision

Every dream I've seen come to pass has been the result of sowing financial seed for it. In chapter 2 I wrote about my personal vision from August 2006. What I didn't mention was that I invested financially for each dream before they materialized in my life.

1. A Television Broadcast

I gave the best seed I had for my dream of having a successful Christian broadcast. I was specific about what I believed God to make happen in our viewer response to the show. Since I gave, our response has far surpassed what the experts deem "a successful broadcast."

2. Books

I gave a significant financial gift to a successful Christian authors organization. I believed that I would see my books in the same bookstores. Today, our books are on the top sellers' list with our publisher.

3. Conferences with a Theme

I gave a large financial gift to my mentor, Joyce Meyer, who hosts women's conferences across the world. I invested this way in order to launch my own conferences. I started out in a mid-size church auditorium with about 350 women. Currently, I am renting convention centers.

4. Helping Troubled Teens

I gave the best gift I had to Mercy Ministries (an organization committed to helping and housing teenage girls who are pregnant, have eating disorders, suffer from abusive pasts and who are victims of human trafficking). As a result, I have been able to consistently give thousands of my books, CD messages, and dream notebooks to girls' homes around the world!

5. A Mission in France

When God began to speak to me about making a difference in France, my first move was to give a financial gift to pastors in Paris. My books are now in the largest bookstores in that beautiful city.

192

I can't say this enough about God's faithfulness. When you choose to operate in God's laws and invest in your future by sowing, He will make a way for your dream to come to pass.

What are you willing to give for your dream? Time? Money? Talent? A ride? A compliment? Encouragement? What can you invest to see your desires come to pass? You might say, "But, Terri, I don't have much to give." Trust me, I understand. Be encouraged that the size of your seed isn't important; it's the significance of the seed.

First Kings 17 records the story of the prophet Elijah who was visiting a widow and her son. There was a terrible famine in the land. God told Elijah to visit a particular widow and she would feed him with cake. (If I were Elijah, I would have run to that house. I love cake . . . it's why I go to weddings!)

When the prophet found the widow, as was customary, he asked for something to drink. Then he asked for something to eat. The widow was reluctant to give him anything because she didn't have much herself. Matter of fact, the drought had wiped her out and all she had to offer was a little bit of flour and some oil. The woman told Elijah that just before he stopped by, she had planned to prepare a meal for her and her little boy, knowing it would be their last.

Elijah replied, "Don't worry about a thing. Go ahead and do what you've said. But first make a small biscuit for me and bring it back here. Then go ahead and make a meal from what's left for you and your son. This is the word of the God of Israel: 'The jar of flour will not run out and the bottle of oil will not become empty before God sends rain on the land and ends this drought'" (1 Kings 17:13, *THE MESSAGE*).

The little the widow had was all God asked for. It wasn't much, but it was significant. As it turned out, the flour and oil she used to make Elijah's cake never ran out. In a time of famine and lack, she had more than enough to eat every single day. Don't hang on to your seed (or eat it). Sow it. The widow gave God her best, and God gave her life. Just imagine what God can do with the best you give Him.

Are you familiar with the story of Jesus feeding many people with some bread and two fish? The Gospel of Mark records that one time Jesus saw a huge crowd and began to teach them. Hours passed. When it was late in the day, the disciples approached Jesus and suggested He send the people off so they could get some dinner. Jesus had another idea. He told them to feed the crowd. The disciples were astonished at the request. *With what?* they wondered. They weren't hauling bags of groceries around and there definitely weren't any catering facilities or restaurants nearby.

When the disciples walked around and took inventory of what the people had, hoping to collect enough food to feed everyone, they came up short. They brought Jesus all they found—five loaves of bread and two fish. That's it. Jesus said, "This is great. It's enough. It's all I'm asking for." Guess what? It was more than enough. Everyone had plenty to eat. There were even 12 baskets of leftovers. Imagine that! (See Mark 6:30-44.)

Think about your vision, your dreams, your goals, your desires. You may be in the early stages of your vision. Right now, your dream may be represented only by a picture stapled to a corkboard or a photo in your journal. Still, you have within your means the ability to invest in your dream. You are never without the seed that will meet your needs. You can sow. Today. Right now.

If you want apple trees in your backyard, you can't just wish them into existence. You can't hope they'll appear one day. You can't speak to the ground and command apple trees to sprout from the soil. You have to sow seed. The same principle applies to the dreams God has for your life. You must sow toward them.

Hebrews 11:1 tells us that faith is the substance of things hoped for, the evidence of things not seen. The *English Standard Version* puts it this way: "Faith is the assurance of things hoped for, the conviction of things not seen." Your giving is a reflection of your faith. How big is your dream? How big is your faith? What kind of investment do you need to make?

You may have heard the statement, "What you make happen for others, God will make happen for you." This is true. When you get involved in sowing toward someone else's dreams, God will send people to sow into your dreams. He will equip you with what you need to make your visions, your dreams, your goals and your desires happen.

195

Giving Challenge

The late Jim Rohn, entrepreneur and motivational speaker, said, "Giving is better than receiving, because giving starts the receiving process."

If you take a look around you, you'll find many people in need. There are organizations, churches, communities, children and families in the United States and all over the world that need help. I believe one of the best things we can do for ourselves, materially and spiritually, is to give. It's not a means to feel proud. Nor does it warrant a pat on our backs. Giving is a means of appreciating how good God is. It's a way of trusting Him with the finances He has provided and will provide. It's a channel to love Him, and to love others the way He calls us to do.

When you give from the heart, you open the doors of heaven to bring forth the resources and opportunities you need to see your dreams happen. I want to challenge you to research places or persons where you can give. Take this a step further and give your best seed. It doesn't have to be a lot of money; it just has to be significant seed—seed that takes sacrifice.

Now keep praying, keep waiting and keep believing. You will experience blessings inside and out as you illustrate the love of God in action.

Chapter 10

GET YOUR EXPECTANCY HIGH

Believe and act as if it were impossible to fail.
CHARLES F. KETTERING

Before my dad ever preached a sermon, the Lord put it on his heart to "act as if" he had a crowd of people listening to him preach. Dad would go as far as preparing the sermon, praying for the people who would one day listen to him, putting his suit on and going into his guest bedroom "as if" he were preaching to thousands of people.

Can you imagine? My dad could! His imagination allowed him to envision thousands of people listening to his every word and being saved, healed and delivered. He could see it so strongly on the inside of him. In order to perfect that image, he acted as if it were already happening. He did this until it actually became reality.

In this final chapter, I want to encourage you to make the ultimate act of faith by expecting that what you have been imagining for your life will come to pass. Just as my father went through the motions of preaching before he ever got behind a pulpit, you can act "as if" to show your determination to reach your dreams.

The second *G* in *IMAGINE BIG* stands for "get your expectancy high." "Do not, therefore, fling away your fearless confidence, for it carries a great and glorious compensation of reward" (Heb. 10:35, *AMP*). There is power in this kind of determined anticipation, but it requires strong faith—a steadfast expectation.

Throughout this chapter we will explore ways to stay focused. You will learn how to grab hold of your dreams, expectations, faith and vision without letting go so God will bring the ideas, opportunities, resources and relationships into the natural realm to make imaginings happen. I'll also offer creative and practical ways you can evidence your expectation.

In chapter 6 we looked at the way our speech manifests both helpful and harmful things in our lives. Let's turn our attention toward the attitudes associated with our speech. Just as you will get what you say, you will also get what you expect, positively or negatively. If you expect to get free from financial bondage, you will have that liberation. If you expect to get promoted, you will advance in your career. If you expect to be healed, you will have physical restoration.

Studies have shown that people who immigrate to the United States are three to four times more likely to become millionaires than those born here.[1] Why is that? It's because the belief that America is a land of opportunity, a place where dreams come true, has been ingrained in their minds. As a result, they come to the United States with the singular focus of finding success. You get what you expect.

A pregnant woman anticipates her child's imminent arrival. She prepares. She fixes up the nursery. She talks about it. She visualizes. Why? Because she's expecting. When you order something online, you check the front door on the estimated delivery date, expecting your package or letter. You don't automatically assume it's not coming. You expect it. You have to change your mindset about your future, your dreams, and the things you have visualized if you have any chance of realizing them. You have to expect to see them come to pass.

To achieve your dreams, you have to believe and act as if you're already doing what you envision. You might even want to think, dress and talk like you've already achieved your goal (the way Jack Canfield and the other guests did at that inspiring party they attended). When you have faith for your dreams, faith sees that dream, faith speaks that dream and faith acts on that dream. When Rodney and I were believing for a baby, I bought announcement cards before I was pregnant. That was an act of faith. I was expecting to get pregnant. I even bought the book *What to Expect When You're Expecting* because I was expecting to be expecting. We were confident that God would give us the desires of our hearts, so we took our faith a step further and acted out our dream.

"My soul, wait only upon God and silently submit to him for my hope and expectation are from him" (Ps. 62:5, *AMP*). You can't truly believe God and not expect anything. When you live by faith, you are expecting something all the time. Your expectancy has everything to do with what you receive.

· · · · ·

199

· · · · ·

Big Faith for Big Dreams

In order to do big things, you have to have big faith—faith that is mature and unwavering. But it doesn't come overnight. You have to learn to develop it and work to maintain it. The following are eight characteristics of faith that work together in building your ability to trust God's working in your life.

1. Faith Hears
God gives us powerful instruction on how to increase our faith: "Faith comes by hearing, and hearing by the word of God"

(Rom. 10:17, *NKJV*). Every single time you hear the Word of God, your faith grows. I've said before that this needs to be a habit, just like brushing your teeth. Most of us wouldn't go a day without brushing, right? Would you ever think of saying, "I've brushed my teeth 300,000 times. Can I stop now?" You could, but that's pretty disgusting, and decay will set in little by little. Our mouths are a breeding ground for germs and bacteria that need to be cleared away each day to protect the health and strength of our teeth.

It's the same with our faith. You could say, "I've been to church nearly every Sunday since I was a child. I've heard the Word at least 3,000 times. Isn't that enough?" You could stop going to church (technically, you can do anything you want), but eventually spiritual decay would set in. Little by little, faith fades when we are not hearing the Word, because we are bombarded with negative elements that try to erode our faith. The best safeguard is hearing God's Word.

2. Faith Sees

Before you can have something, you have to see yourself having it. Before you can do something, you have to see yourself doing it. The dreams I wrote in my book were visions in my mind years before they began happening. Faith always sees the end result before it is reality. When I was a little girl, my parents taught me to see with the eye of faith. That lesson carried me through some tough times in adulthood when I shouldn't have had any hope for something.

For instance, when I couldn't get pregnant for a long time, I saw myself with a baby. I saw myself with a little girl. I even saw her having red hair. I believed God and, eventually, I had Kassidi. It was the same thing with my ministry. Every single time I walked into a bookstore I pictured my book being on the shelves. There came a day when I was browsing in Barnes & Noble and saw my book, just like I had imagined. Today, I even see my books (translated in French) on bookshelves in Paris, France. When you see your dream in your mind, you create a blueprint and you activate your faith to make it happen.

3. Faith Speaks

When God wants something to happen, He speaks it. God said it, and it was so. I have seen studies indicating that the average person talks to herself about 50,000 times a day; 80 percent of that self-talk is negative.[2] We tell ourselves things such as, "They don't like me." "I'm not cut out to play the lead role." "I'll never get that promotion." "I'm a terrible speaker." "I'm always late." "I can never get organized." Any message you allow to fill your head will become what you think about the most.

When your mind focuses on something, it tends to manifest. I remember a particular photo of Rodney and me that was taken during a hard stretch in our marriage. We were on vacation, and we fought the whole time; yet when the camera came out, we were smiling. You would never know we were so broken and hurting. While we were separated, I prayed over this picture daily.

At the lowest point of this emotional hell, I couldn't even look at the picture. I covered it up with my hand while I prayed over it. It took some time for me to actually look at Rodney's face, and more time after that to say his name. But eventually, I did. I prayed, "Thank You for healing my marriage. Thank You that nothing is too big for You. You specialize in doing the impossible, and I trust You to heal my marriage." But it wasn't enough.

Though we may confess and believe for our dreams, sometimes we speak against them in ways we don't realize and therefore limit or prevent change. Case in point: I would thank God for healing my marriage but then call my best friend and complain, "Ugh! I can't imagine ever being back with him. Our relationship is never going to work!" We have to speak what we believe, not what we feel. No matter how impossible your dreams look, trust God for them, then leave them in His hands and do not speak against them. That's how you release faith through words.

4. Faith Acts

When my nephew Preston was a little boy, Jesse Duplantis prophesied over him. He said that he would be able to play several musical instruments. Preston could actually see himself playing the guitar and the drums. He would talk about it constantly and tell people, "Brother Jesse said I'm going to play a bunch of instruments." But faith doesn't stop there. It also acts. Preston had to take lessons and practice the instruments.

Faith without works is dead. You have to do something. I couldn't just say, "In Jesus' name, I'm going to have books in bookstores." I had to write a book, whether I had a publishing contract or not. I needed to act to make my dream happen and be ready when opportunity came.

5. Faith Stands

Faith is simply trusting God. It is confidence that what you believe is true without having evidence of its existence. One time the Lord said to me, "Say that you trust Me with an exclamation point, not a question mark." Point taken! We can't tell God we trust Him but question His ability to pull off the impossible. We can, however, say something like, "I have no idea how You're going to do this, but I trust that You can and You will!" That's confidence.

When I was on the cheerleading squad in high school, I was always at the top of the pyramid moves. One time, the team decided to try something new. The pyramid was three people high and, as always, I was at the top. The dismount required me to flip backward into the arms of my teammates below. As adventurous as I was, I was nervous. My knees were shaking, and I was looking around where my catchers stood, making sure someone was there. When I finally dismounted, my coach came up to me. "Terri," she began. "You look stupid. You have fear written all over your face. You're not going to entertain the crowd, because they'll be nervous just watching you." She paused for a moment. "What's the problem? Don't you trust your teammates to catch you?"

No, I didn't. I was scared.

That day, our coach instituted a verbal contract that the girls would do their part and catch me, and I would trust them to follow through on what they were there to do. It built up my courage. My confidence started to grow. When game day came, I was able to climb up to the top of the pyramid and dismount, knowing there was nothing to fear.

How much more can we trust God? Read the following verses from the Bible about absolute trust: In Romans 4:21, Abraham declared that he was "fully persuaded that God had power to do what he had promised." Second Corinthians 5:7 reminds us that "we live by faith, not by sight." Second Timothy 1:12 states, "I know in whom I have believed." You can't be full of fear and full of faith at the same time, so stand firm and trust God.

6. Faith Rejoices

My dad says, "The greatest expression of your faith is praise." I like to think of praise as a gate opener. You may be familiar with Psalm 100:4: "Enter his gates with thanksgiving and his courts with praise." *THE MESSAGE* version reads as follows: "Enter with the password: 'Thank you!' Make yourselves at home, talking praise." When you praise God in advance of the dream you are waiting for, you push open the gate and walk right into the presence of God. When you lift your hands and thank Him, you open the lines of communication so God hears you. He delights in praise and worship, because it proves you trust Him.

7. Faith Sows

From the beginning of time, God gave human beings two things—authority and seed. He has given you authority to determine your destiny by the seeds you sow. When we plant the seeds of faith by giving, we take another step that leads to the harvest of our dreams.

In 2007, I was praying for France and my dream to start a ministry outreach there. I didn't know a thing about ministry in that part of the world, nor did I have any connections or invitations to preach there. But I did have a dream. I found a picture of a church in France where I wanted to speak, and I put it in my dream book. I researched. I prayed. I sowed. Since then, I've taken annual outreach trips to France and preached in many different cities in the country. But I had never preached in that one particular church. Recently, I felt I needed to invest again in that one dream. I felt God telling me to double my seed. I obeyed. Less than two weeks after my investment, God opened the door for me in that particular church. God is faithful. He always rewards obedience. He always rewards faith.

8. Faith Rests

Here's a revelation I had not long ago. Satan only attacks you three times: (1) when you wake up, (2) when you go to bed at night, and (3) every minute in between. As soon as you wake up, he tries to poison you with negative messages: *It's never going to happen. You're not qualified. Those dreams are stupid.* As soon as your head hits the pillow at night, he takes advantage of your weary mind: *You really messed up today. You didn't finish what you set out to do. Tomorrow will be just as bad.* And he keeps up the attack throughout the day. You have to have faith, be strong in the Word and trust God during these battles. You need to learn to rest in God and allow Him to come through for you.

One of my heroes from the Bible is Jehoshaphat. In 2 Chronicles 20, two armies come against this man. He's outnumbered, overpowered and doesn't know what to do. Then he drops to his knees and begins worshiping God. God delivered him. When the devil attacks you with fear, fight back by worshiping God. Rest in Him. Be still and allow God to fight your battle.

· · · · ·

205

· · · · ·

Expect to See New Dreams Happen

When you can confidently trust God in the midst of impossibility, towering mountains and seemingly unconquerable obstacles, your faith is big enough for the dreams He has put on your heart.

I want to encourage you with how God-imaginings and expectancy will bring about big dreams. Let's revisit my dream of ministering in France. When the idea first entered my mind, I sprang into action. I began praying over that nation every single day. I imagined taking a group of ladies from our ministry to Paris every year. I imagined my books being translated in French. I imagined teaching there. I bought a map of France at my local craft store, framed it and hung it in my office to keep before my eyes. I also sowed $500 to some pastors in Paris because they were already making an impact in France, and I wanted to join my faith with theirs. I took further action and wrote a mini-book called *You're Valuable to God* (*Vous Avez de la Valeur aux Yeux de Dieu*). I began to share my vision with others who helped support my dream financially. I did all of these things because I expected God to fulfill my dream.

To date, we have given away 15,000 copies of my French mini-book all over the streets of Paris, on the metro, in the cafés and to the Parisian artists of Sacre Coeur. I have spoken in some of the largest churches in France (as many as 11,000 members), as well as in cities such as Paris, Marseille, Nice, Toulon, Vichy and Brest. I even have a French publisher who prints and stores all my French resources and has sold out of my books.

My vision for France now is so much bigger. I've written it down, and I look at it daily. I don't know how God is going to do it, but I'm believing in Him. I know He can help me accomplish these dreams. He's done so much already. I expect to see my new dreams happen.

Fight for Your Dreams

As you keep the image of your dreams before your eyes and act and wait in expectation, you will have to fight for them. They are not going to happen without some effort. You will have to battle against fears, procrastination, negative messages from outside, and internal forces and attacks of the devil. You will never, ever outgrow warfare; you must simply learn to fight. This is a truth you must take to heart.

My dad loves boxing. I've never understood the sport and I still don't get it. Growing up, whenever a match was on TV, I would go in the study and try to watch it with my dad as a bonding experience. One time, I noticed that in the middle of throwing punches, the opponents started hugging (at least that's what it looked like to me). I told my dad, "Hey, these guys have mixed emotions. It's like they hit and then they hug. Then they go back to hitting, and then they hug again. I'm confused. Do they like each other or not?" I'm sure Dad was laughing on the inside, but he simply said, "Honey, I think your mom is calling you in the kitchen."

"No, she's not," I said, pouting.

With a wink in his eye, he craned his head toward the other room and said, "Yes, she is. Can't you hear her now?"

"But, Dad! No one ever calls me to the kitchen!" (Anyone who knows anything about my cooking skills—or lack thereof—can verify it's true.)

Unlike me, my sister, Jerri, was a huge boxing fan. For some reason, Jerri always enjoyed boxing me. We laugh about it now, but there were times we would get into an argument and our verbal battles would turn physical. Jerri would punch me repeatedly, but I wasn't the type to fight back. I'd just let out a big, "Ow!"

She'd punch me again and try to provoke me further, "C'mon, Terri, hit me back."

I'd practically be in tears. "No, it hurts!" Jerri would keep them coming, daring me to return the blows.

One particular time, she was "sparring" with me when I escaped by running to my bedroom. I flopped facedown on my bed and tried to hide under the covers. Jerri was tough. Nothing held her back. Not even a cozy comforter. She pounded my little body over and over while I yelled out, "Stop it, Jerri, it hurts. Leave me alone." She refused to quit until I hit her back. "Fight me, Terri. Do it!" At some point, she gave up. She let out an exasperated sigh and headed toward the bedroom door, saying, "You're no fun." As she was about to step into the hall, something came over me. Game on.

207

I sprang out of bed, made a dash toward my sister and planted a powerful punch right in the middle of her back, knocking her down. It was a proud moment for me. "Ooooowwww," Jerri cried out. We both started laughing.

Obviously, I am not comparing my sister to the devil, but consider whether you have allowed the devil to pound you over and over without defending yourself. Have you just lain there helplessly taking his assault? You need to learn how to fight back. You have to start throwing punches his way. You must determine not to give up.

Abraham Lincoln was faced with many opportunities to give up on his dream of being president of the United States. Between the ages of 22 and 24, he failed in two separate business ventures. During that time, he also ran for state legislature and lost. Two years later, the woman he loved died, and that was followed by a nervous breakdown. Over the next 20 years, Lincoln lost 7 more political races. Finally, at 51 years old, Abraham Lincoln was elected president of the United States. He made it. He achieved his dreams. Many people would have stopped pursuing this particular dream after so many failures, but not Lincoln. He fought for his dream no matter what. His tenacity helped him become one of the most revered and respected leaders of the United States. Every time you see a penny, be reminded to fight for your dream.

Scripture tells us, "For a dream comes with much business and painful effort" (Eccles. 5:3, *AMP*). In other words, it's not going to be easy. I say it again: *You will never outgrow warfare; you must simply learn to fight*. I used to have a hard time accepting that statement. Over the years, I've taken a bunch of personality tests, and all of them indicated my tendency for an easygoing nature. I am a pacifist at heart and want everybody to get along and have fun.

I even wondered why the devil has to be so mean. Why can't he just leave us alone? But John 10:10 tells us that Satan is around only to kill, steal and destroy. It is not in his nature to leave us alone, much less get along with us. There is never a time in your life when he feels sorry for you. There is never a time when he feels he might have been too hard on you and should ease up a little. He has one plan for you—to steal, destroy and kill. Satan is trying to knock you down. You have to learn to fight. Stop allowing him to back you into a corner. Get into the middle of the ring.

What are you believing God for today? What dreams come to mind? What imaginings has God put on your heart? Are you believing for good health? To get married? Have a baby? Get the job of your dreams? Build a homeless shelter? Have your own talk show? Buy a nice home for your family? Whatever image you are keeping before your eyes, fight for it until it comes to pass. Anticipate the enemy's blows. Know that he is coming after you and arm yourself with the spiritual weapons God lists for us in Ephesians 6. Fight the good fight and come out victorious, enjoying the fruits of a dream realized.

Who Is in Your Corner?

As you expect your dreams to come to pass, you need to surround yourself with supportive and positive people who will encourage you to press onward. First, train with a good coach. Find someone to speak words of life and truth over you. Get a mentor who will teach you to stand firm in your faith.

Years ago, I went through a period where I lost my dreams, my marriage was falling apart and I had no vision for my future. I didn't know what in the world God wanted to do with me. I just wanted to give up on life.

I began listening to some Joyce Meyer CDs. She became my coach, my mentor. Did I have a face-to-face session with her? No. Did I hang out with her and ask her a bunch of questions? No. But she spoke truth into my life because she rode around with me in the car. She did laundry with me. She talked while I got ready in the morning. Every day I listened to her and was encouraged, inspired and motivated. She taught me to stop letting emotions make my decisions. She taught me I was in the mess I was in because of a series of mistakes and, to turn things around, I would need to make a series of right choices. The more I soaked in God's Word through her sermons, the brighter the light of truth shined in my spirit.

Find an inspiring mentor and absorb his or her faith-building messages. It doesn't matter who it is as long as he or she is teaching you biblical truths. I can even be your coach. Pick up my books and some CDs, or download podcasts and let me speak into your life. Part of my purpose is to help others fulfill theirs. I would love to help you focus on your dreams and realize your vision, even if it is from a distance through the amazing technology we have available today.

Second, hang out with friends who are uplifting, support-ive and keep you accountable. Ever watch a boxing match and notice there's always somebody in the corner of the ring en-couraging the boxer? They're not yelling, "You stink, man. You're a loser. You'll never win." No, they're always building up these fighters. One of the most important jobs of the "cor-ner man" is to keep his man refreshed. He offers water. He wipes the sweat off the boxer. He provides motivation. He re-minds the fighter to keep fighting because he can win.

I've got many "corner women" in my ring. My friend Theresa has been backing me since 1985. She is always building me up when I need it and warning me when I'm veering off the right path. She prays for me and reminds me of what God says. Another amazing friend, Donna, has been in my corner since 2000. She works with me at the office and is always cheering me on. She holds me accountable and tells me what I need to hear, good or bad, to help me stay focused on my dreams. Lucy is another corner woman who travels with me and keeps me spiritually aware of what's going on when I start feeling fatigued. Sandi is my "big dreamer" friend who confidently assures me that my dreams are totally possible, and she encourages me to not even blink an eye at a closed door. I love them all so much.

Who do you hang out with? Who do you spend the most time with? Who is in your corner? Remember, you are who you hang out with. That's why it's so important to spend time with people you admire, respect and look up to. If you want to be successful, hang out with successful people. If you want to be a visionary, spend time with visionaries. If you want to experience your dreams, surround yourself with dream makers. Don't clutter your life with people who can't offer you support for your dreams or who aren't moving toward their own goals. They won't bring anything positive to your life and may keep you stuck.

211

Anchor or *Motor*?

I've read in Jack Canfield's book *The Success Principles* that there are two types of people you will encounter in your life—anchors and motors. Anchors are heavy and stationary and will weigh you down. Motors, however, are on the move and going somewhere; so it's wise to stick with them. Which type of people do you have around you? How can you change the influences in your life?

1. Make a list of the people you spend time with on a regular basis—family members, co-workers, neighbors, church friends and social acquaintances.

2. Go through the list and put a minus sign by the names of those who are negative and toxic, and a plus sign by the ones who are positive and encouraging.

3. Compare the lists. Are there any patterns? Are there more anchors than motors? Or vice versa? Think about the roles these people play in your life and how you can change the impact they have.

4. Begin seeking out the people on your list who bring positive energies to your life, and avoid those who pull you down. Start to weed out those who drain you and keep you from what God wants you to do.

Don't Get Distracted

Expecting your dreams to come to pass and fighting for them requires intense focus. The reason most people fail is because they get distracted. Satan is a deceiver and is out to distract you from your dreams. He does this in many different ways. I want to offer three of the main areas where he has the easiest time creating the most havoc.

1. Time

One of the most common ways Satan distracts us is through time. How much time has passed since you started believing for your dream? You might think, *Too much!* Well, the devil will try to convince you that your dream is never going to happen because too much time has slipped by, so you might as well give up. I recently received a message from someone who said he had believed for something for a year and experienced no change or breakthroughs. This man sounded so frustrated, it made me think of how happy Satan must be to see his response. He delights when others are discouraged. A lapse of time is a big reason that we have lapses in faith. Don't let the enemy convince you it's too late. Remember, we are on God's time, not ours, the world's or the devil's. Our dreams will come true when He says it's time.

2. People

Remember the story of Samson and Delilah (see Judg. 16)? Delilah was strategically sent from Satan to distract Samson. She appealed to his pride and convinced him to rebel against God. Consequently, she robbed him of the power God bestowed on his life. Samson was the strongest man who ever lived, but he went down in history for his weakness. Satan will do the same thing in your life. Whether someone is pushing you in the wrong direction, distracting you from your goals or dragging you down, the devil will use people to get you off track.

3. Your Past

Satan has been keeping a file on you. He's been watching you since the day you were born, observing every mistake you make and keeping note of it. As soon as you start dreaming for great things, he drags up this file of your past to remind you, "Aren't you the girl who had the abortion?" "So how many guys have you slept with again?" "Wait a minute. Didn't you cheat on your wife last year?" The devil uses your mistakes to make you feel unworthy of God's blessings. He wants you to forget that the moment you repent, God forgives you and remembers your sins no more. While it's easy for God to forgive us, sometimes we have a tough time forgiving ourselves. We have to stop remembering what God has forgotten. It doesn't matter how bad you've messed up, God can still do something with your life. Don't let Satan distract you from your future by dredging up your past.

Satan has nothing but time to work on you. He will send all sorts of distractions to throw you off course. You have to be on your guard, always building up your faith to combat his efforts. Don't allow him to be successful or give him the satisfaction of seeing you delay your dream one more second.

Never Throw in the Towel

Don't give up the struggle and quit the fight. Don't walk off the battlefield without achieving the victory. The enemy wants you to throw in the towel where your kids, your marriage, your financial situation and your dreams are concerned. I heard somebody once say, "It's *always* too soon to give up." I love that statement. You should never give up on your dreams. The apostle Paul said he fought the good fight and finished the race (see 2 Tim. 4:7). We should strive to do just that—finish exactly what God called us to do.

As we journey into our dreams, there are times when we will feel overwhelmed. We may feel ill-equipped to stay in the fight, but that's when we have to turn our eyes toward heaven and remember that God is in our corner. He is fighting alongside us in any battle He calls us to fight. He did it for David when he battled Goliath, and He'll do it for you. God is most glorified when the underdog conquers the mighty enemy. He wants you to win, and He wants you to complete your purpose. Never feel that you are too small or weak or unworthy to take on an opponent if God calls you to it.

Have you ever given much thought to the referees in professional sports? I'm always amazed how, armed only with a whistle, one average guy can stop a raging bull of a linebacker from charging. In boxing, a ref can send a heavyweight champion back to his corner. What is so powerful about this little guy that he can control these giants? Well, he's not operating in his own power. When the ref blows his whistle, that linebacker knows the NFL stands behind the ref. When that boxing match is raging and the referee calls "time out," the entire Boxing Federation is backing him.

It's time to blow the whistle in your life and say, "Devil, enough is enough, I am now calling on the name of Jesus. I am not giving up." When you invoke the name of Jesus, you have just grabbed heaven's attention and commanded a host of angels at your side. You have just caused Satan to cover his ears, screaming, and run in the opposite direction.

What are you believing God for? Good health? Financial stability? A broken marriage made whole? A lucrative business? Children who are committed to serving God? A promotion? Imagine the possibilities that exist for you today and for your future. Know that God will meet you if you have faith in Him. You can count on Him. You can expect that some way, somehow, someday, God will make your dreams, your vision and your goals become realities.

What Are You Expecting?

We began this journey by allowing ourselves to just imagine. It may have been the first time you did something like that since childhood.

In chapter 1, I asked you to make an "I WANT" list. Now, as we are closing the final pages of this book, I want you to think about those things you put on your list and then write down what you are believing God for today. Maybe they're the same. Maybe they've changed. Use the space below to write out what you are expecting. Make a list of the things you know God is working on for you, and rejoice in them.

216

CONCLUSION

If you want to view paradise, simply look around and
view it. Anything you want to, do it. Want to change the world?
There's nothing to it.
WILLY WONKA

I built an acronym from the words *IMAGINE BIG* to take you through the steps of the process of identifying your dreams, connecting with them daily, taking action to make them happen and trusting God to lead you to them.

The process of reclaiming your imagination if it has lain dormant might feel a bit intimidating, a little foolish at times and maybe even confusing at first. But it is also a thrilling experience that will help you learn more about yourself and draw closer to God. When you know that your dreams and visions are aligned with God's plan for your life, not only will you feel invigorated by the possibilities open to you, but you will also achieve more in every aspect of your life because you know where you are going.

Being able to *imagine your future* is one of the greatest gifts you will ever receive. It is what gives you purpose and direction. *Making a dream book* is almost like taking that gift and covering it in beautiful gift-wrapping paper so you have a present to yourself to open every day. When you *assign time each day* to spend with your dreams, you are treating that gift as something more than a pretty knick-knack to place on a shelf. You are making use of it in every way possible. This is a God-given blessing that many people never receive throughout their lives, so don't take it for granted and don't set it aside for another day.

Get your goals in place and *initiate the action* necessary to give life to your dreams. Be confident in what God has purposed for you and go after that vision with everything that's in you. You will most certainly find God waiting there for you to help you achieve what you've set out to do. No matter how outrageous your dreams may seem to others, when God has given them to you, He will equip you with what you need to make them happen.

Get rid of negative thoughts and spoken words that distract you from God's promises. Fill your mind and your mouth with positive talk. Even when things look bleak and it doesn't seem your dream will come to pass, give thanks to God. *Continually express your gratitude to Him for how faithful, amazing and wonderful He is.* Praise Him even for the things you imagine that have not yet appeared.

Trust the desires God places in your heart as you seek Him and His will. Focus on your God-given imaginings and watch as your desires and your efforts to bring them about intensify. Kick up your faith by making an investment. *Sow seed for your dream with a grateful heart, and expect the unlimited blessings* He has in store for you.

At the opening of the conclusion, I quoted a couple of lines from the song "Pure Imagination" from the classic film *Willy Wonka and the Chocolate Factory.* I want you to think about this for two reasons. First, the entire message of that story is keeping a dream in front of you, giving yourself permission to let your imagination run wild at any age, and never letting anyone discourage you from believing anything is possible. Second, the song suggests that if you want to change the world, it is as easy as deciding that is what you are going to do.

With God, it really is that simple. You can change the world a lot, or just in your little area, but you can accomplish the impossible because God has placed you here with a purpose. He has something He intends for you to do. Find out what that is. Use your imagination and dream of where you can meet God to do great things.

ENDNOTES

Chapter 1: Imagine Your Future

1. Merriam-Webster, "imagination." http://www.merriam-webster.com/dictionary/imagination.
2. Napoleon Hill, *Think and Grow Rich!* (New York: Aventine Press, 2004).
3. The Hebrew verb "meditate on" (*hagah be*) also means "imagine" and "devise (in the mind)" according to F. Brown, S. R. Driver, and C. A. Briggs, *A Hebrew and English Lexicon of the Old Testament* (Oxford: The Clarendon Press, 1951), p. 211.
4. Keith Moore, *A Vision of Victory* CD series.
5. Jack Canfield with Janet Switzer, *The Success Principles* (New York: William Morrow Paperbacks, 2006).
6. David Schaefer, "Visualizing Accelerates Goal Achievement," ArticlesBase, August 20, 2008. http://www.articlesbase.com/motivational-articles/visualizing-accelerates-goal-achievement-529621.html.
7. Jack Nicklaus, quoted in "Advanced Sports Psychology," Winner's Mind. http://winnersmind.co.uk/from_visualisation_to_hallucination.htm.
8. Jack Canfield with Janet Switzer, *The Success Principles* (New York: William Morrow Paperbacks, 2006), p. 85.
9. Dr. Seuss (Theodor Geisel), *Oh, the Places You'll Go!* (New York: Random House, 1990).
10. Kenneth Hagin, quoted in Jerry Savelle, *Prayer of Petition: Breaking Through the Impossible* (Ventura, CA: Regal, 2011).
11. John Maxwell, *Today Matters: 12 Daily Practices to Guarantee Tomorrow's Success* (New York: Center Street, 2005).

Chapter 2: Make a Dream Book

1. Jim Carrey, interview on the *Oprah Winfrey Show,* 1997. http://www.quotationspage.com/quotes/Jim_Carrey/.
2. "Lou Holtz," The Richardson Company. http://www.rctm.com/Products/louholtz.htm (accessed June 2012).
3. Jack Canfield with Janet Switzer, *The Success Principles* (New York: William Morrow Paperbacks, 2006), p. 89.
4. Ibid., p. 88.
5. Napoleon Hill, *Think and Grow Rich!* (New York: Aventine Press, 2004).
6. Jack Canfield, Mark Victor Hansen and Les Hewitt, *The Power of Focus* (New York: HCI, 2000), pp. 77-78.

Chapter 3: Assign Time Daily to Review Your Dreams

1. Jack Canfield with Janet Switzer, *The Success Principles* (New York: William Morrow Paperbacks, 2006), p. 89.
2. Jack Canfield, Mark Victor Hansen and Les Hewitt, *The Power of Focus* (New York: HCI, 2000), p. 51.
3. Jack Canfield with Janet Switzer, *The Success Principles* (New York: William Morrow Paperbacks, 2006), pp. 93-94.
4. Clark LV. "Effect of mental practice on the development of a certain motor skill." *Research Quarterly*, v31 n4 (Dec. 1960):560-569.
5. Jack Canfield with Janet Switzer, *The Success Principles* (New York: William Morrow Paperbacks, 2006).

6. Published by A&M Publishers 600, rue Pierre-Caisse, C.P. 40013 St-Jean-sur-Richelieu, QC, Canada, J3A 1L0.

7. http://www.nielsen.com/content/dam/corporate/us/en/reports-downloads/2011-Reports/Nielsen-cross-platform-report-Q1-2011-reissued.pdf.

Chapter 4: Get Goals in Place

1. Jack Canfield with Janet Switzer, *The Success Principles* (New York: William Morrow Paperbacks, 2006).

2. Ibid.

3. Napoleon Hill, *Think and Grow Rich!* (New York: Aventine Press, 2004).

Chapter 5: Initiate Action Now

1 "Steven Spielberg: Synopsis," A&E Biography, 2012. http://www.biography.com/people/steven-spielberg-9490621.

2. Julie Morgenstern, *Time Management from the Inside Out* (New York: Henry Holt and Company, 2004), pp. 27-32, 34-35.

3. Jack Canfield with Janet Switzer, *The Success Principles* (New York: William Morrow Paperbacks, 2006), p. 105.

Chapter 6: No More Negativity

1. Daniel G. Amen, M.D. "ANT Therapy: How to Develop Your Own Internal Anteater to Eradicate Automatic Negative Thoughts," Ahha Self-help Articles Collection. http://ahha.org/articles.asp?Id=100.

2. Jim Carrey, quoted in Jim Randel, *The Skinny on Willpower* (New York: RAND Media, 2009), January 22.

3. Jack Canfield with Janet Switzer, *The Success Principles* (New York: William Morrow Paperbacks, 2006).

4. Ibid.

5. John Maxwell, *Failing Forward* (Nashville, TN: Thomas Nelson, 2007).

6. Adapted from *Rear Admiral Robert E. Peary, Civil Engineer Corps, US Navy*, produced by the Navy Office of Information, Internal Relations Division, OI-430, January 6, 1964. http://www.history.navy.mil/bios/peary_roberte.htm.

7. "Oscar Clendenning Hammerstein II," Encyclopedia.com. http://www.encyclopedia.com/topic/Oscar_Hammerstein_2d.aspx.

8. Marion Davis, "Larry Luckless No More: Whatever Happened to . . . ?" NY Daily News, May 7, 1995. http://articles.nydailynews.com/1995-05-07/news/17964595_1_social-security-breathing-construction-site.

9. http://www.statisticbrain.com/new-years-resolution-statistics/

Chapter 9: Invest in Your Dreams

1. Rick Warren, *The Purpose Driven Life* (Grand Rapids, MI: Zondervan, 2002), p. 257.

Chapter 10: Get Your Expectancy High

1. http://addicted2success.com/success-advice/video-nido-qubein-why-immigrants-are-4x-more-likely-to-become-millionaires/ and http://www.christianpost.com/news/zig-on-the-immigrants-attitude-47681/

2. Dr. Alice Domar Ph.D, Clinical Psychologist [stresscourse.tripod.com/id101.html]

ABOUT THE AUTHOR

For years, Terri Savelle Foy's life was average. She had no dreams to pursue. Each passing day was just a repeat of the day before. Finally, with a marriage in trouble and her life falling apart, Terri made a change. She began to pursue God like never before, developed a new routine and discovered the power of having a dream and purpose.

As Terri started to recognize her own dreams and goals, she simply wrote them down and reviewed them consistently. This written vision became a road map to drive her life. As a result, those dreams are now a reality.

Terri has become the founder of an international Christian ministry. She an author, a conference speaker and a success coach to hun-dreds of thousands of people all over the world. Her bestselling book, *Make Your Dreams Bigger than Your Memories*, has helped people discover how to overcome the hurts of the past and see the possibilities of a limitless future.

Terri Savelle Foy is a cheerleader of dreams and is convinced that "if you can dream it, God can do it." She is known across the globe as a world-class motivator of hope and success through her transparent and humorous teaching style. Terri's unique ability to communicate success strategies in a simple and practical way has awakened the dreams of the young and old alike.

Terri shares from personal experience the biblical concepts of using the gift of the imagination to reach full potential in Jesus Christ. From stay-at-home moms to business executives, Terri consistently inspires others to go after their dreams. With step-by-step instruction and the inspiration to follow through, people are fueled with the passion to complete their life assignment down to the last detail (see John 17:4).

Terri and her husband, Rodney Foy, have been married since 1991 and are the parents of a beautiful redheaded daughter, Kassidi Cherie. They live near Fort Worth, Texas. For more information about Terri, go to www.terri.com.

FURTHER RESOURCES FROM TERRI SAVELLE FOY

TERRI.COM

- Weekly Video Podcasts
- Product Specials
- Video/Audio Downloads
- Tour Dates
- And Much More

Terri Savelle Foy Ministries
P.O. Box 1959 Rockwall, TX 75087

LEAVE YOUR PAST IN THE PAST!

Make Your Dreams Bigger Than Your Memories
ISBN 978-1-9421-126140

Holding on to the past and all its mistakes will only hinder you from taking hold of the future that God has planned for you. But it can be so hard to let it go! That's why you must dream extraordinary dreams. When you focus your mind and heart on reaching your God-given goals, the past cannot hold you prisoner any longer. In *Make Your Dreams Bigger Than Your Memories*, Terri Savelle Foy shares her personal journey out of a painful past into total freedom and walks with you, step by step, along the path to God's purpose for you. Your past does not define your future . . . so stop living as if it does! Turn your back on guilt, shame and regret to face the reality of God's love and the promise of His plans for you.

This is a life-changing book—one of the best I have ever read!
NANCY ALCORN
Founder and President, Mercy Ministries International